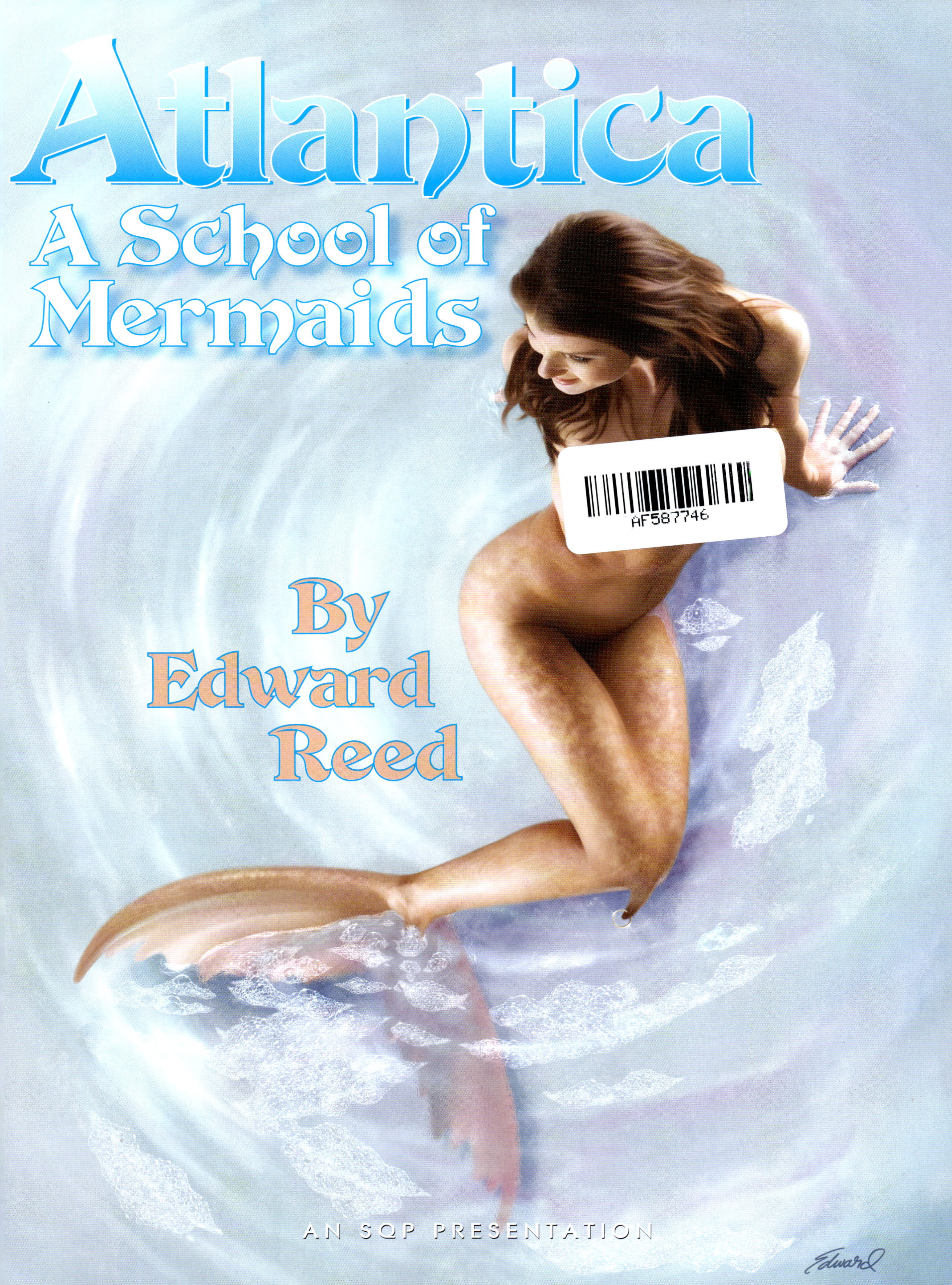
Atlantica
A School of Mermaids
By
Edward
Reed
AN SQP PRESENTATION
Edward

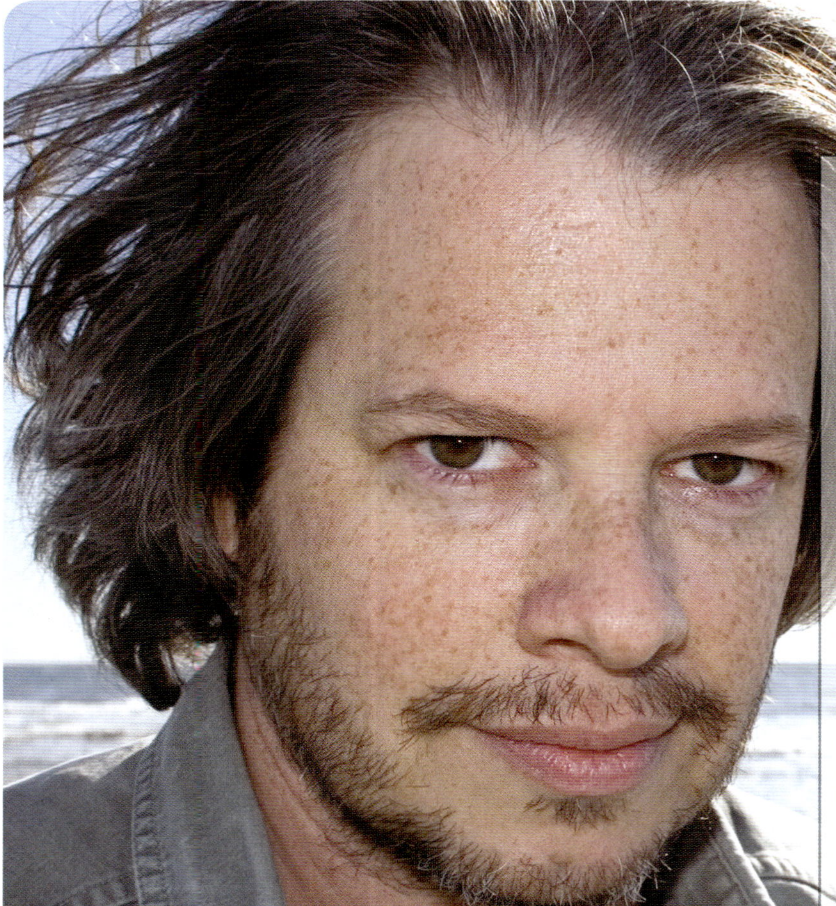

Edward Reed

Illustrator, Photographer, Mermaid Rangler

Living near a body of water is something I cannot imagine my life without. As a kid I grew up near large lakes, roaring rivers and the occasional little pond where I would try to catch frogs and turtles and for the past 32 years I have lived near the ocean. I have walked the beaches of the Atlantic Ocean, the Gulf of Mexico, the Pacific Ocean and even the South China Sea but sadly I cannot say I have ever seen a mermaid. For hundreds of years thousands of mariners have sailed Earth's seas. Lonely, delirious and delusional they dreamed of those left behind. They sought treasure, glory and fame. Some claimed to have seen mermaids...

These digitally created paintings were completed using Corel Painter X and a Wacom Intuos Tablet on a Mac Pro Quad-Core Intel Xeon but for this project to be fully realized I also had to become a photographer and work with local models so a Canon Digital Rebel XT, a few studio light soft boxes and a large photo backdrop were added to my arsenal. Photography isn't my specialty so I mostly I relied on other photographers to help me with reference material for these mermaids therefore I would like to give special thanks to photographer Marcus Ranum (www.ranum.com) and his models Sarah Ellis (www.modelsarah.com) and Rael Cohen. Also much thanks to photographer Jiri Matula and the models at Smartnet IBC Ltd and Sophie Collier of Lockstock at DeviantArt.com. I would especially like to thank Peggy-Lee Thomas and Ashley Spalding for posing for me and being such fantastic models by overlooking my inexperience as a photographer! A huge thank you to Sal Quartuccio and Bob Keenan for believing in me and taking a chance on an amateur illustrator that dreamed for many years of being a part of the elite SQP artist lineup!

Most importantly I thank my wife Amy for dealing with my staying up to the wee hours of the morning and sleeping in late for 3 years to complete this project! This body of work wouldn't exist without the help, guidance and patience of those special persons mentioned here.

For thousands of years the mermaid has been an alluring part of cultural myth in every part of the world and now, from the oceans of my imagination I present to you my own delirious vision of mermaids in repose

– *Edward Reed*

For the very latest on Edward Reed's work, please visit

www.edwardreed.com

About the Artist:

Edward Reed is the former editorial advisor and contributing editor for *Airbrush Art + Action magazine* and *Art Scene International magazine* and is currently represented by **Creative Design Outlet** (creativedesignoutlet.com) for digital distribution of images for online PSP taggers.

Edward currently resides in Summerville, South Carolina with his gorgeous wife and two beautiful daughters.

Edward

Atlantica - A School of Mermaids

Book design by Grassy Knoll Studios.

Published by SQP Inc.
PO Box 248 - Columbus NJ 08022
Sal Quartuccio & Bob Keenan - Publishers

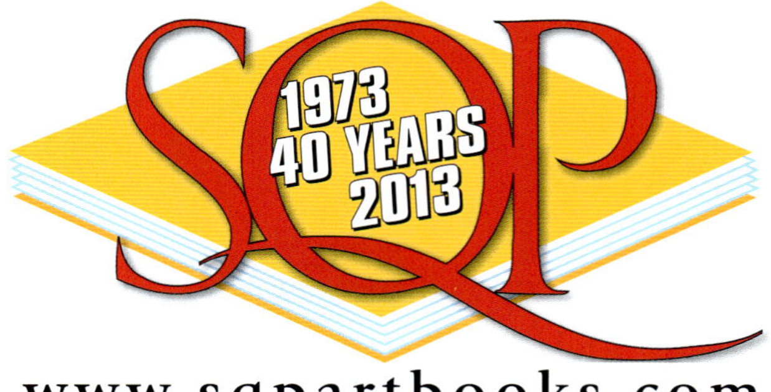

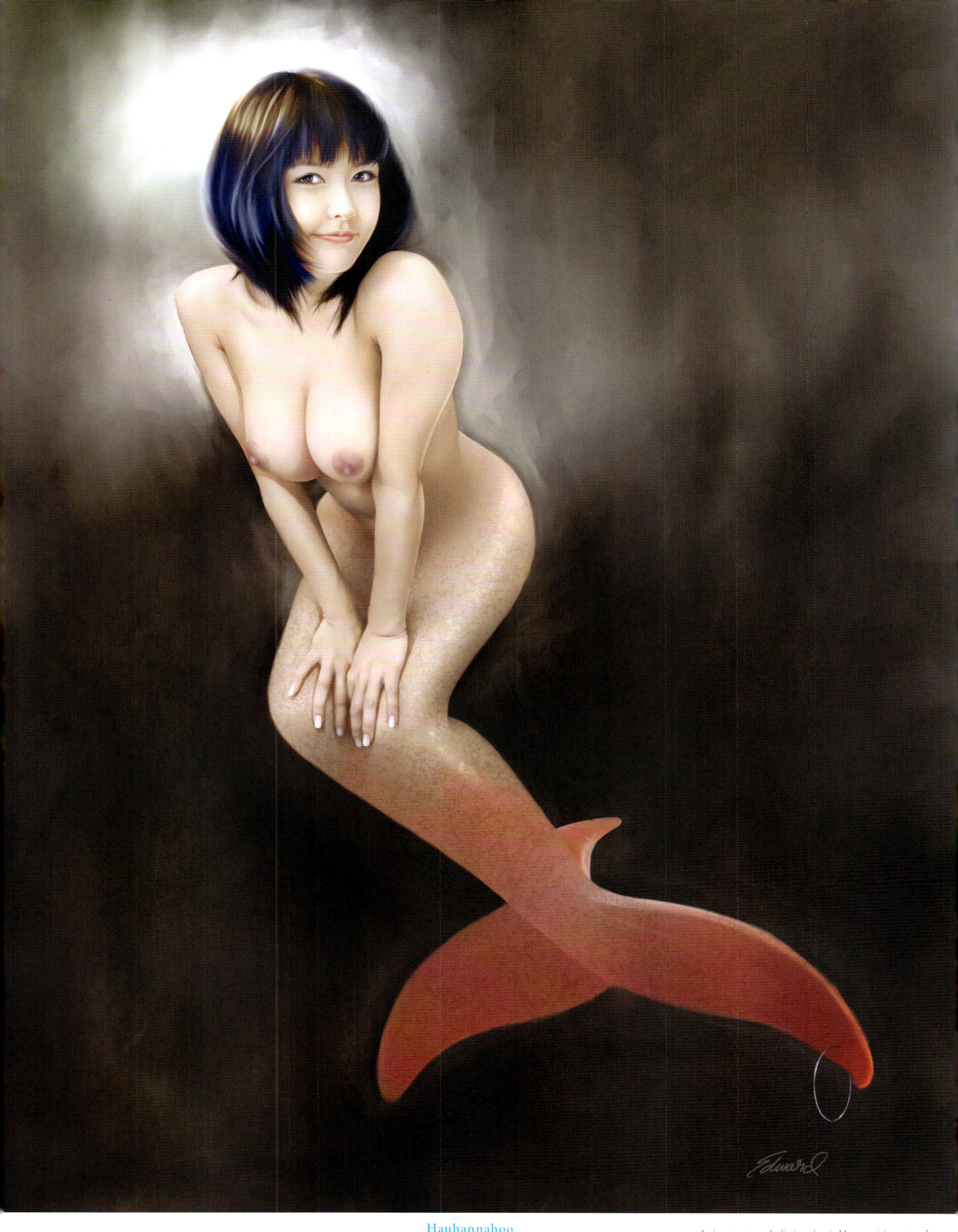

Hauhannahoo

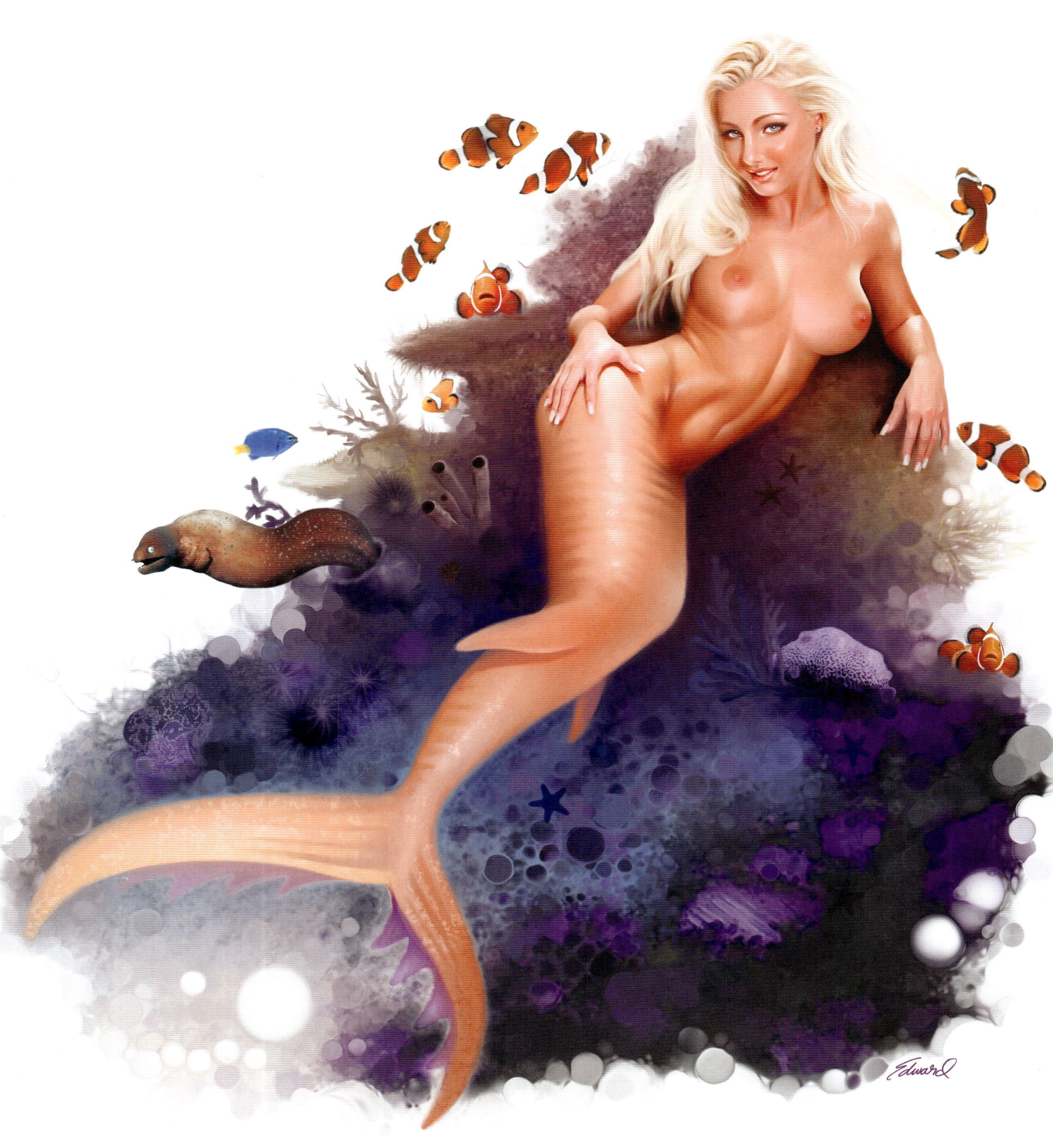

Coral

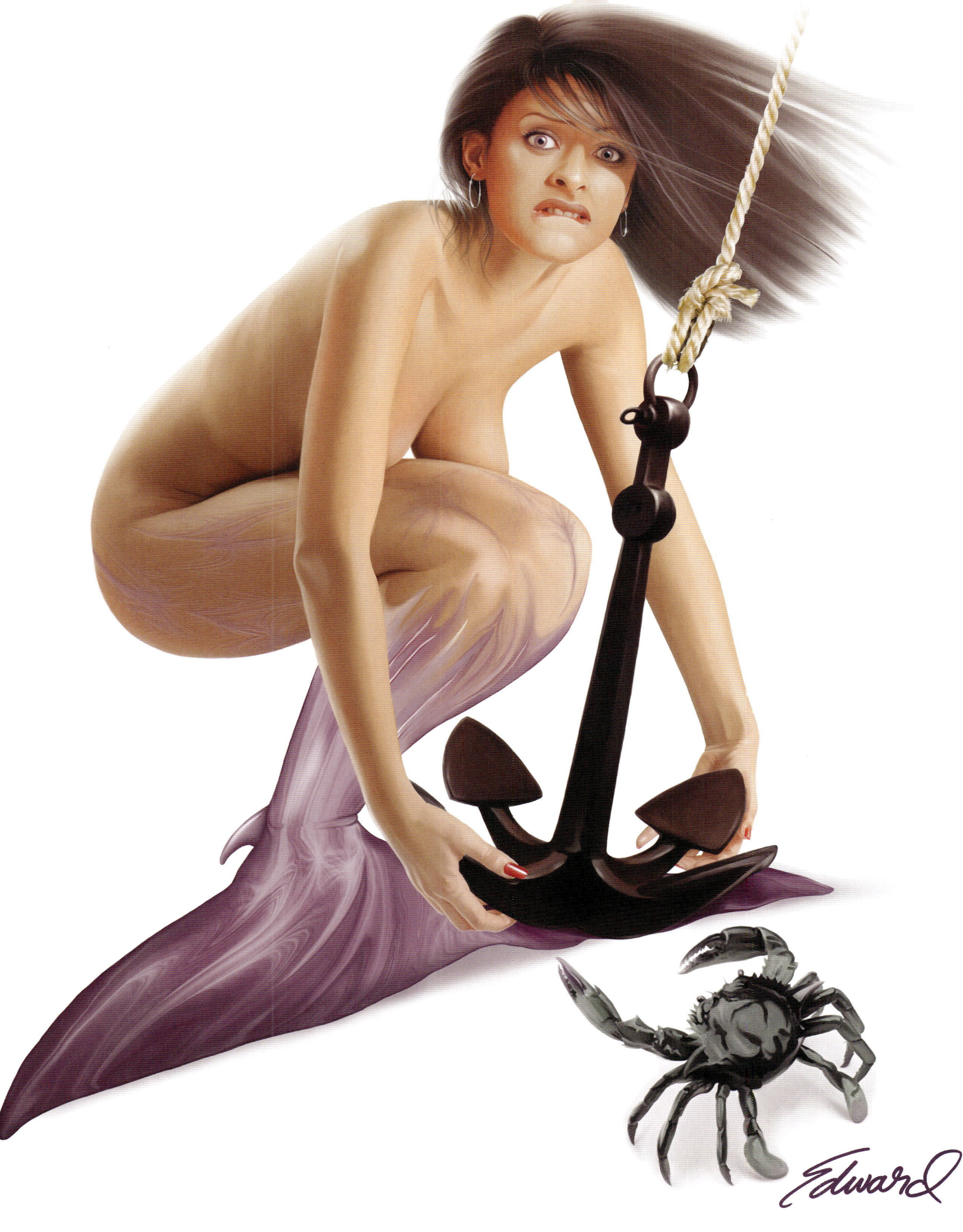

Anchors Away

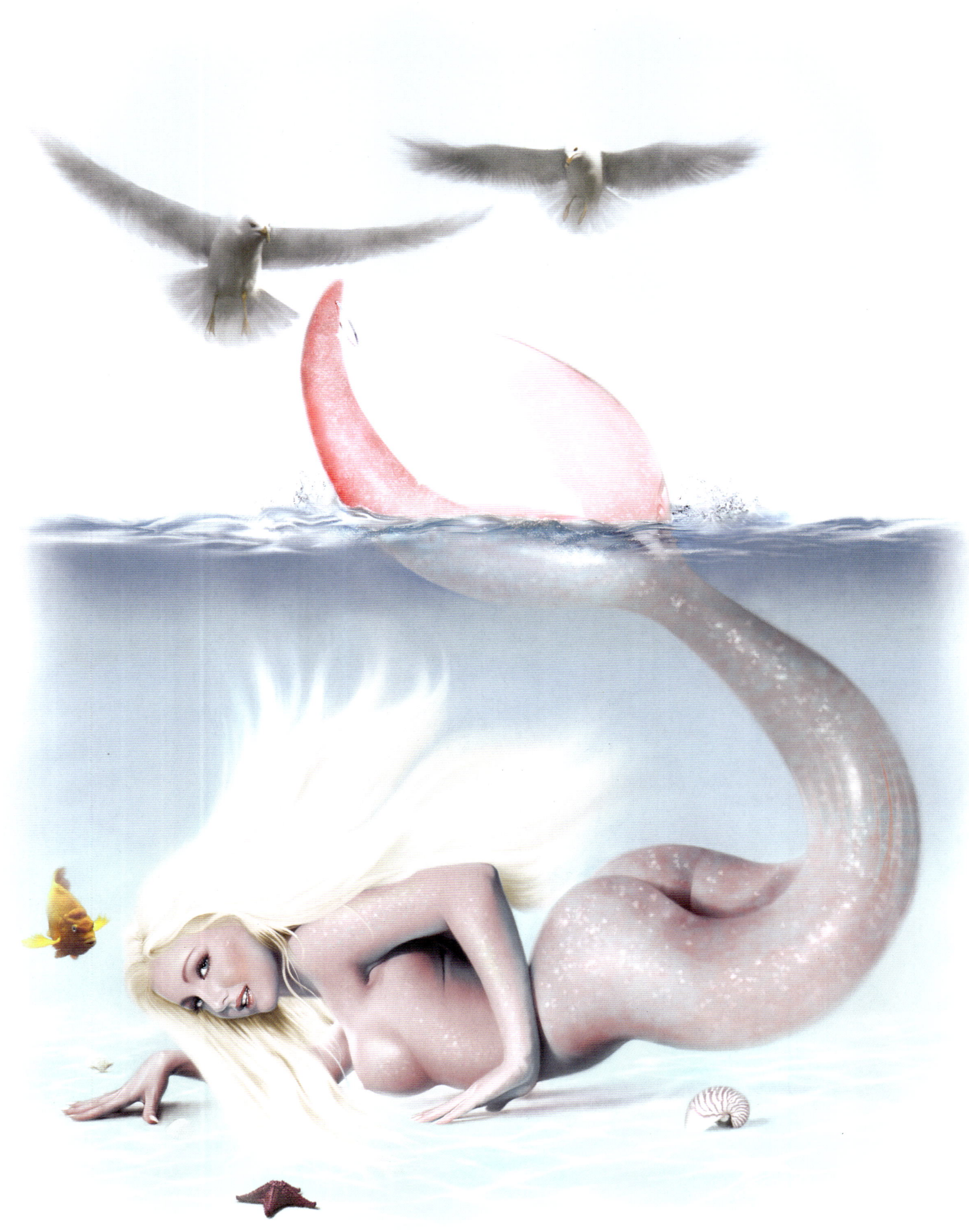

Splish-Spash

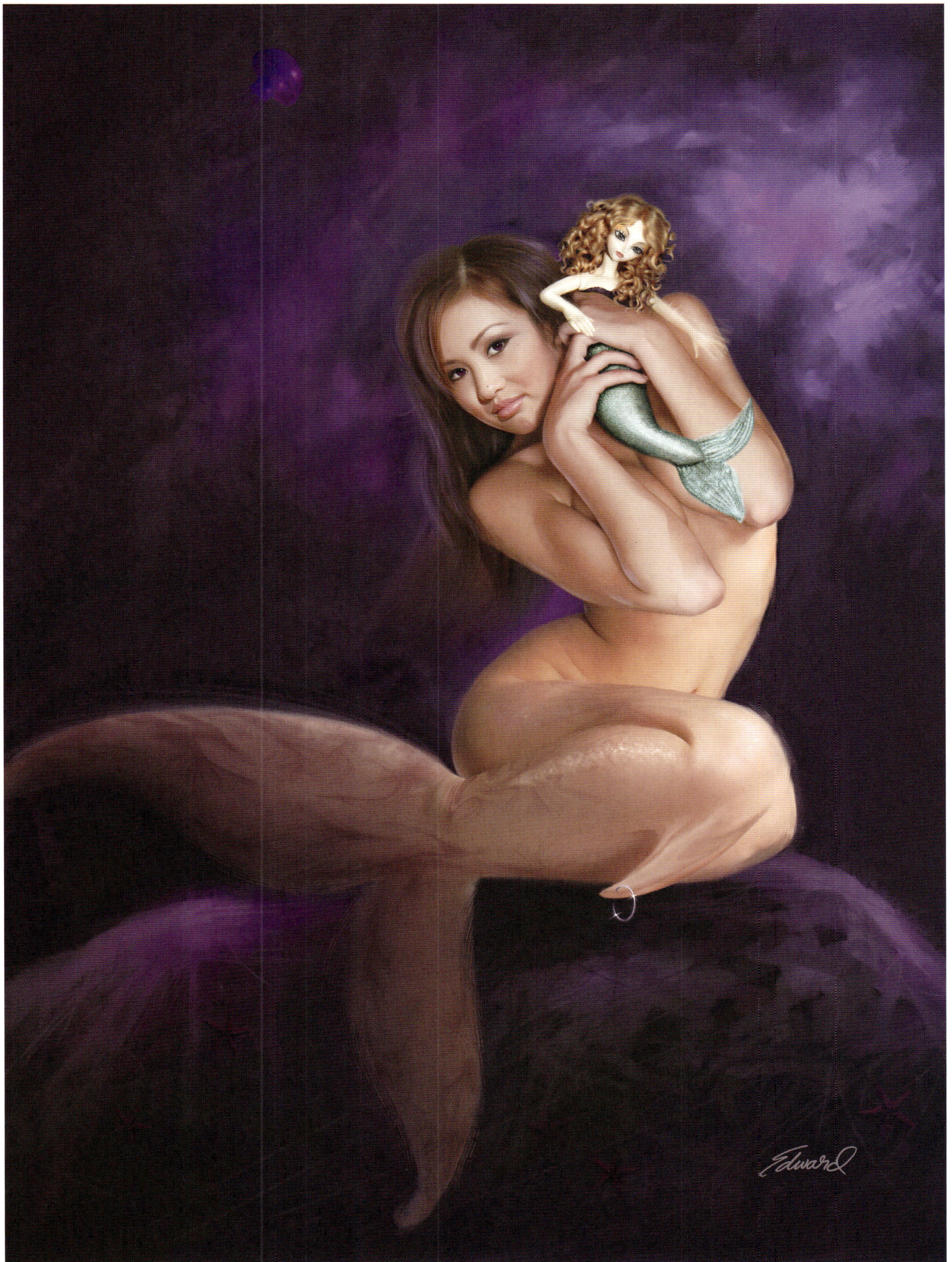

Moon Jelly

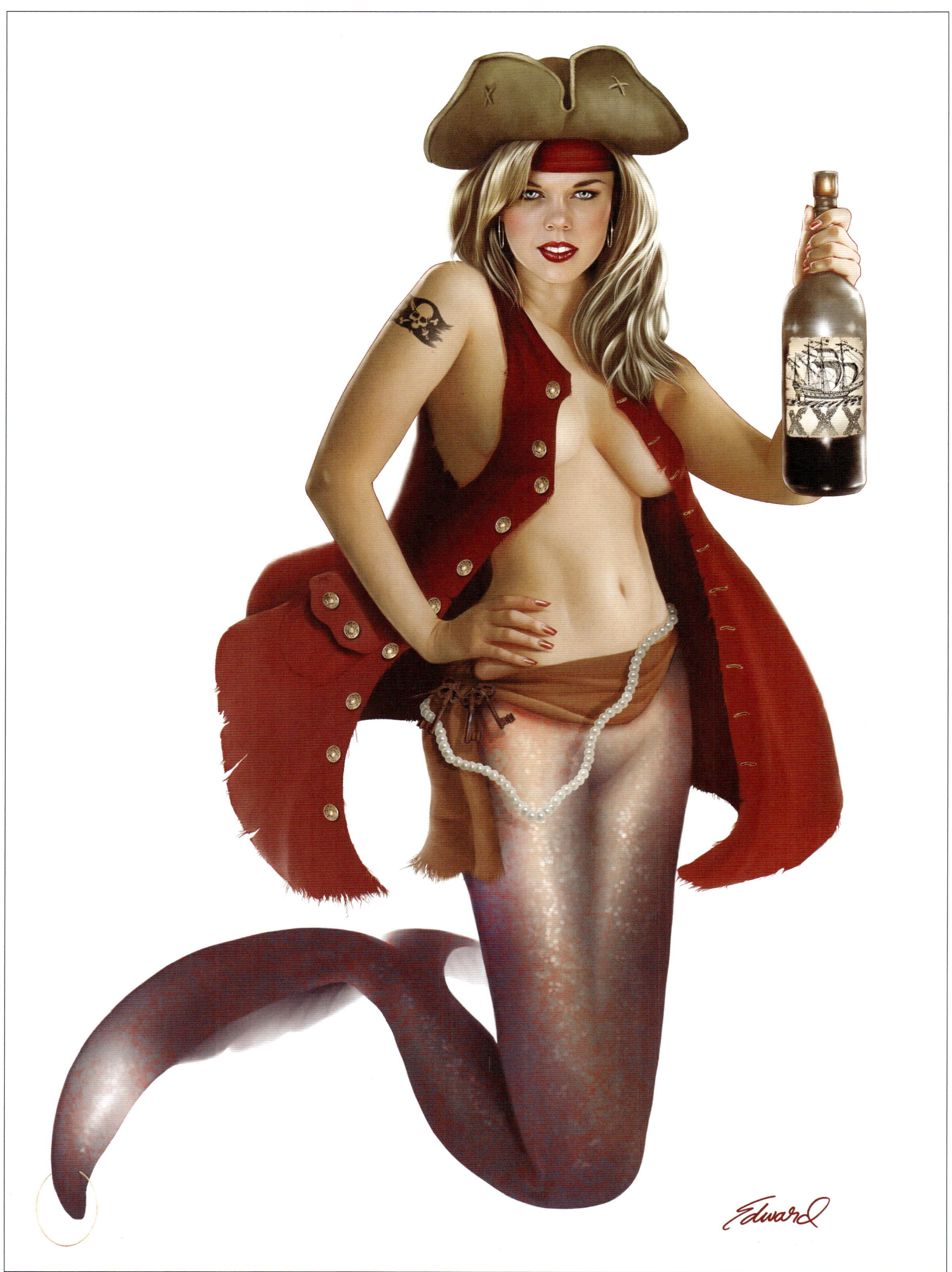

...And a Bottle of Rum

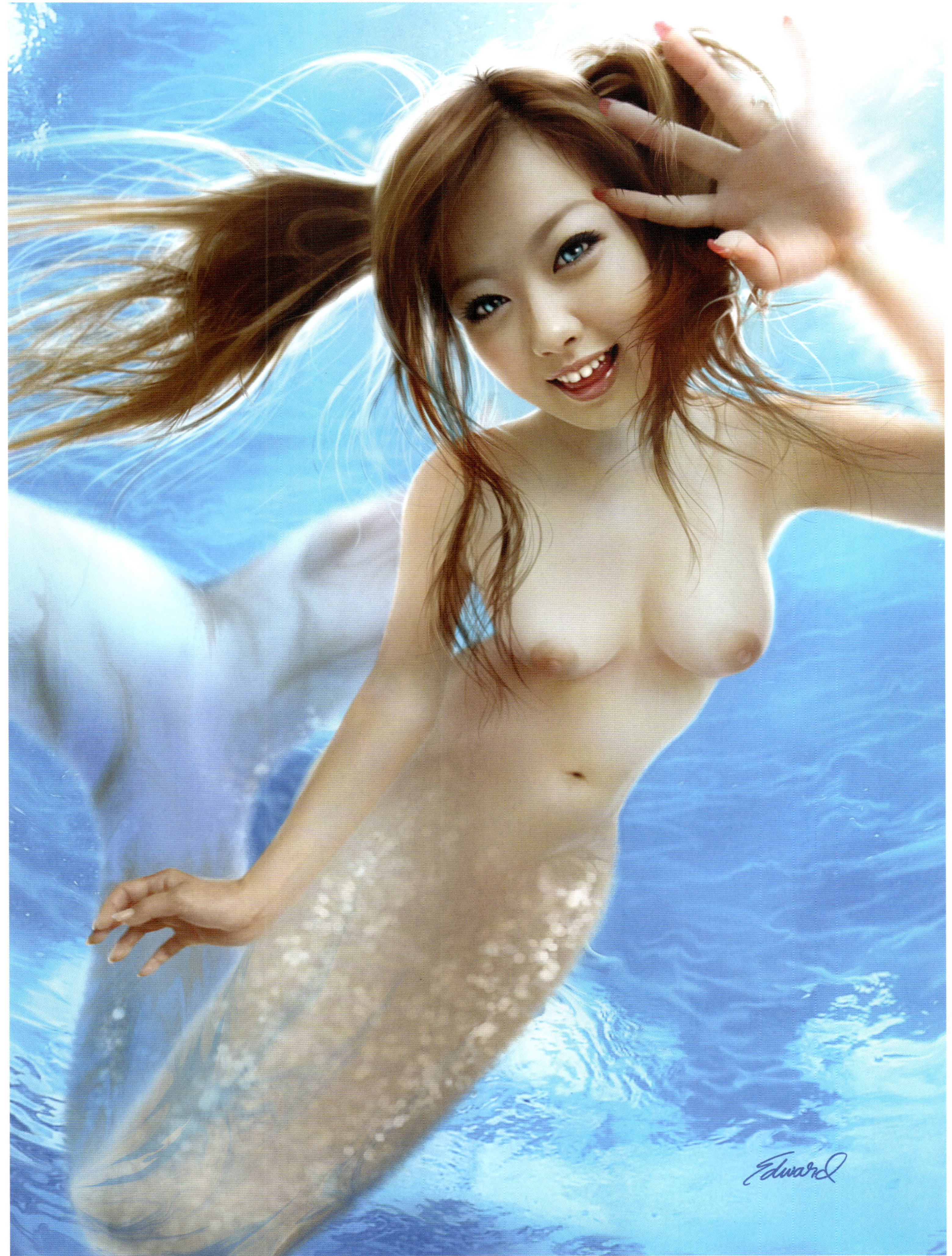

Tantan

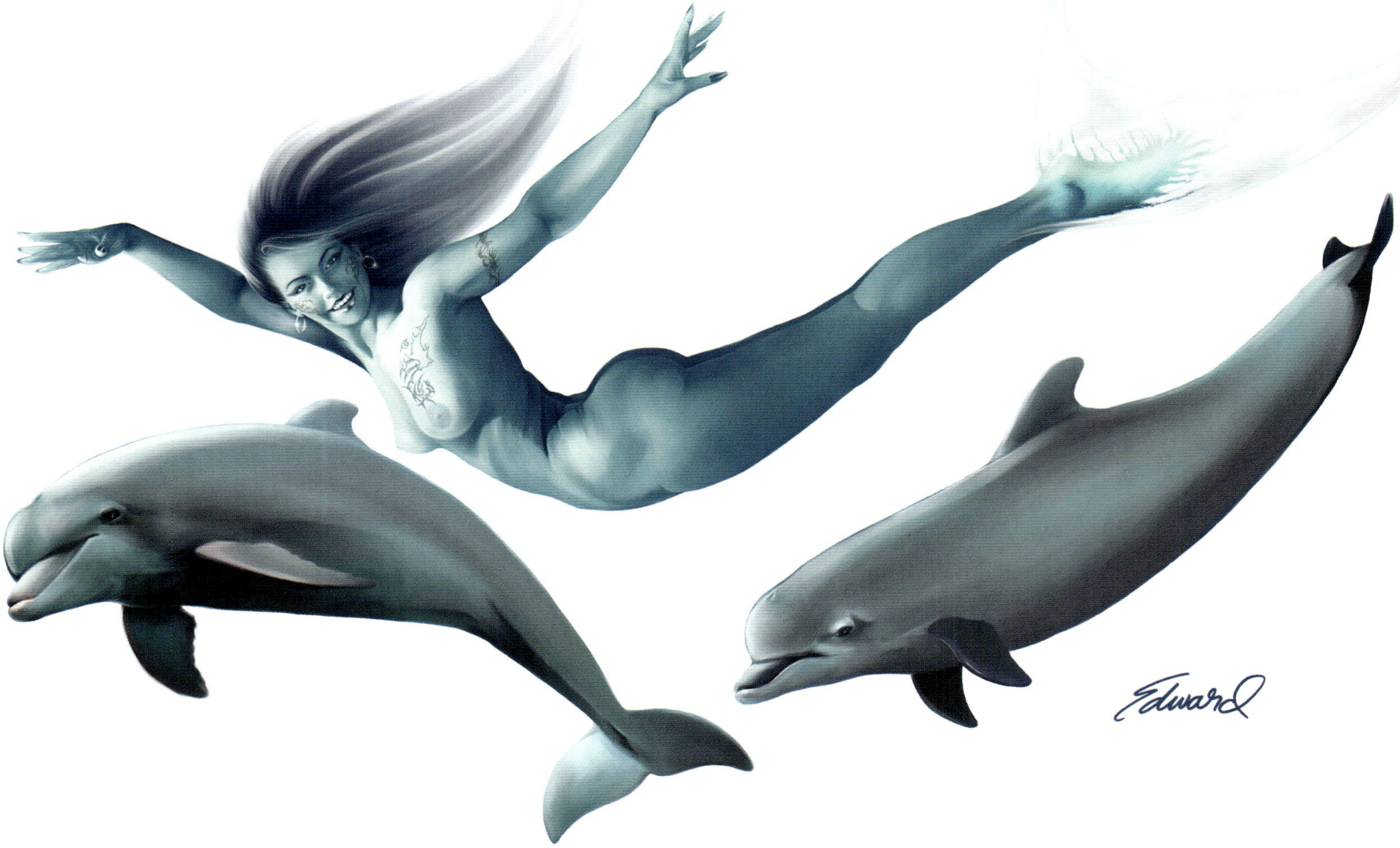

Jelly Fish

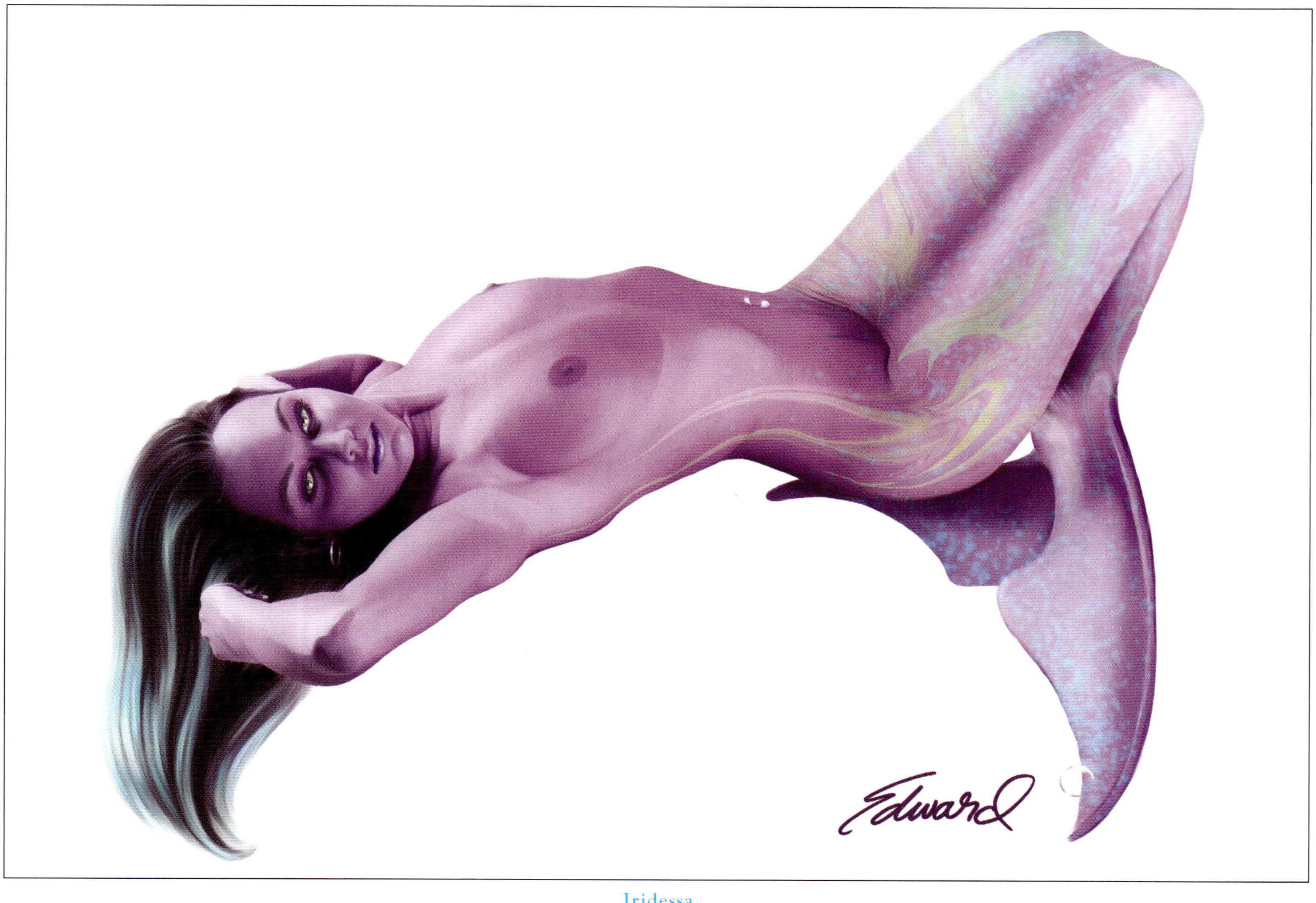

Iridessa

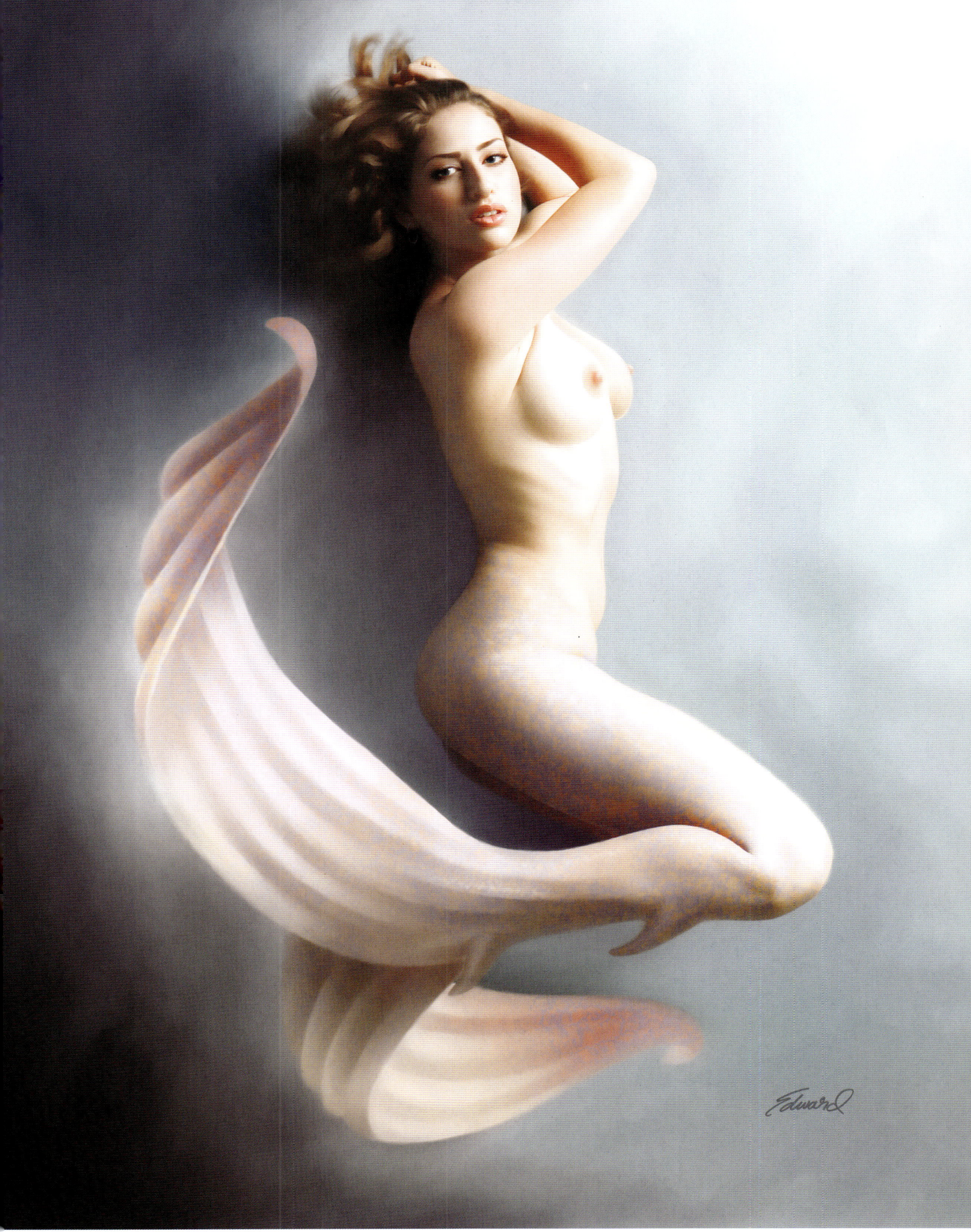

Syrena

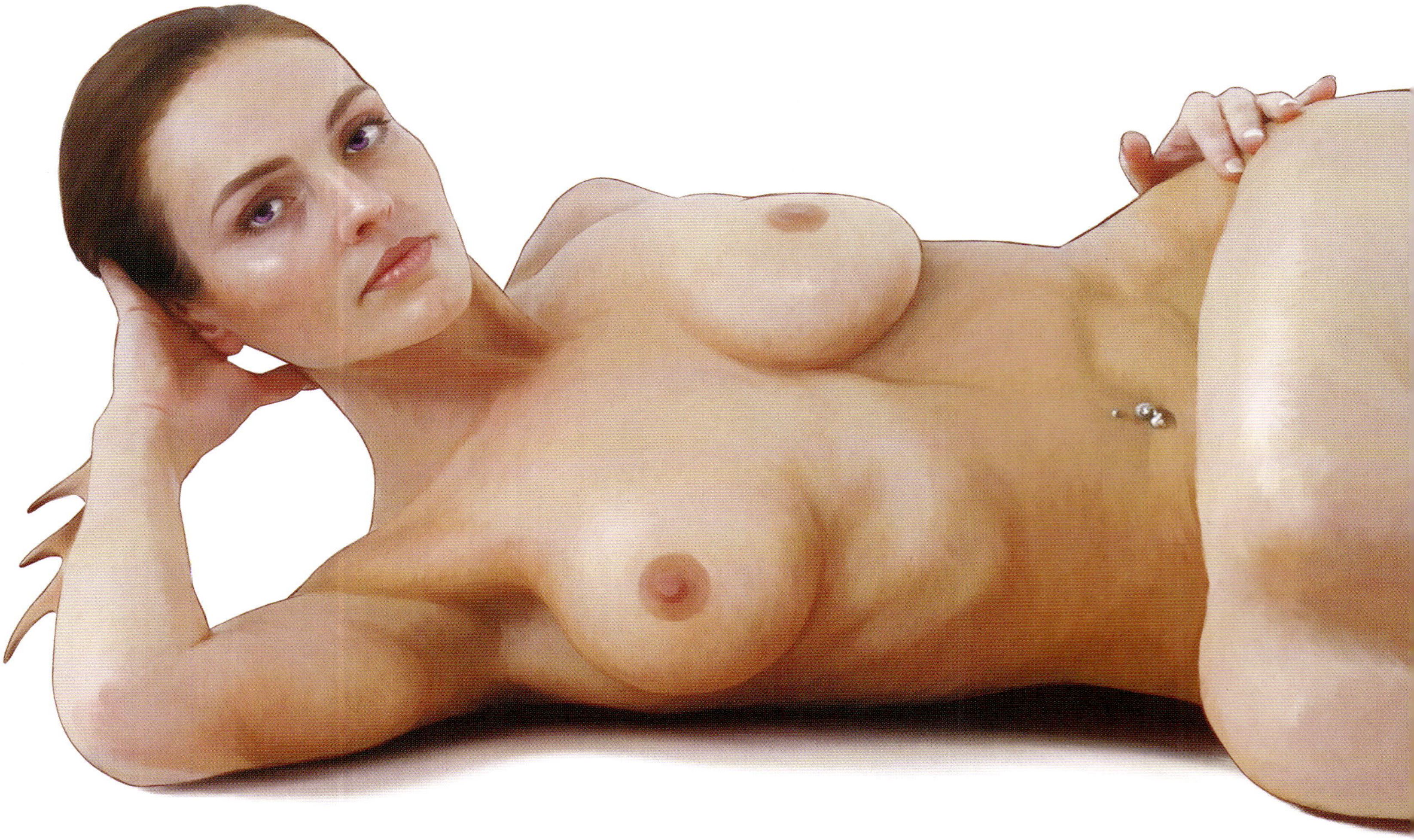

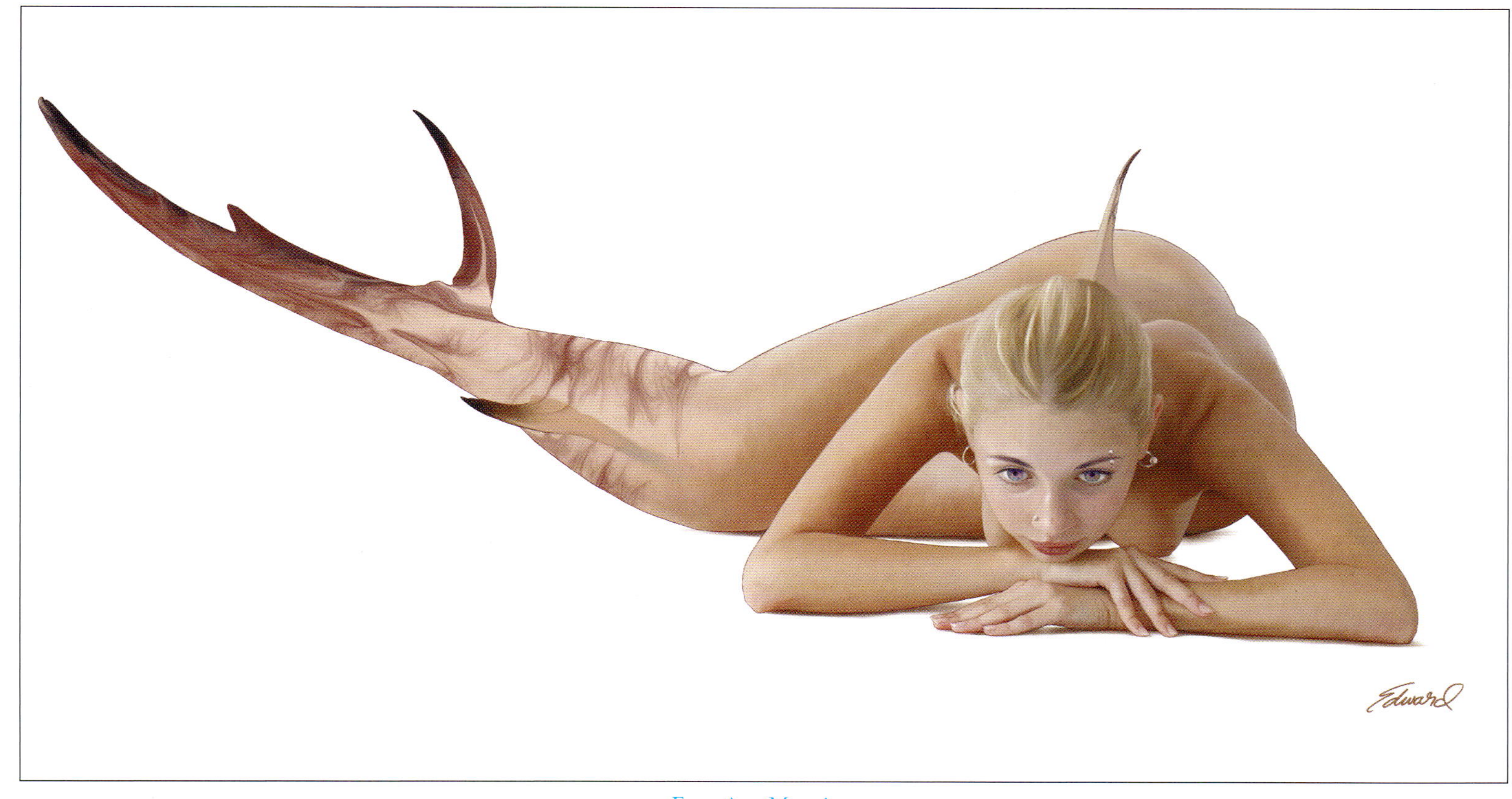

Eyes Are Mosaics

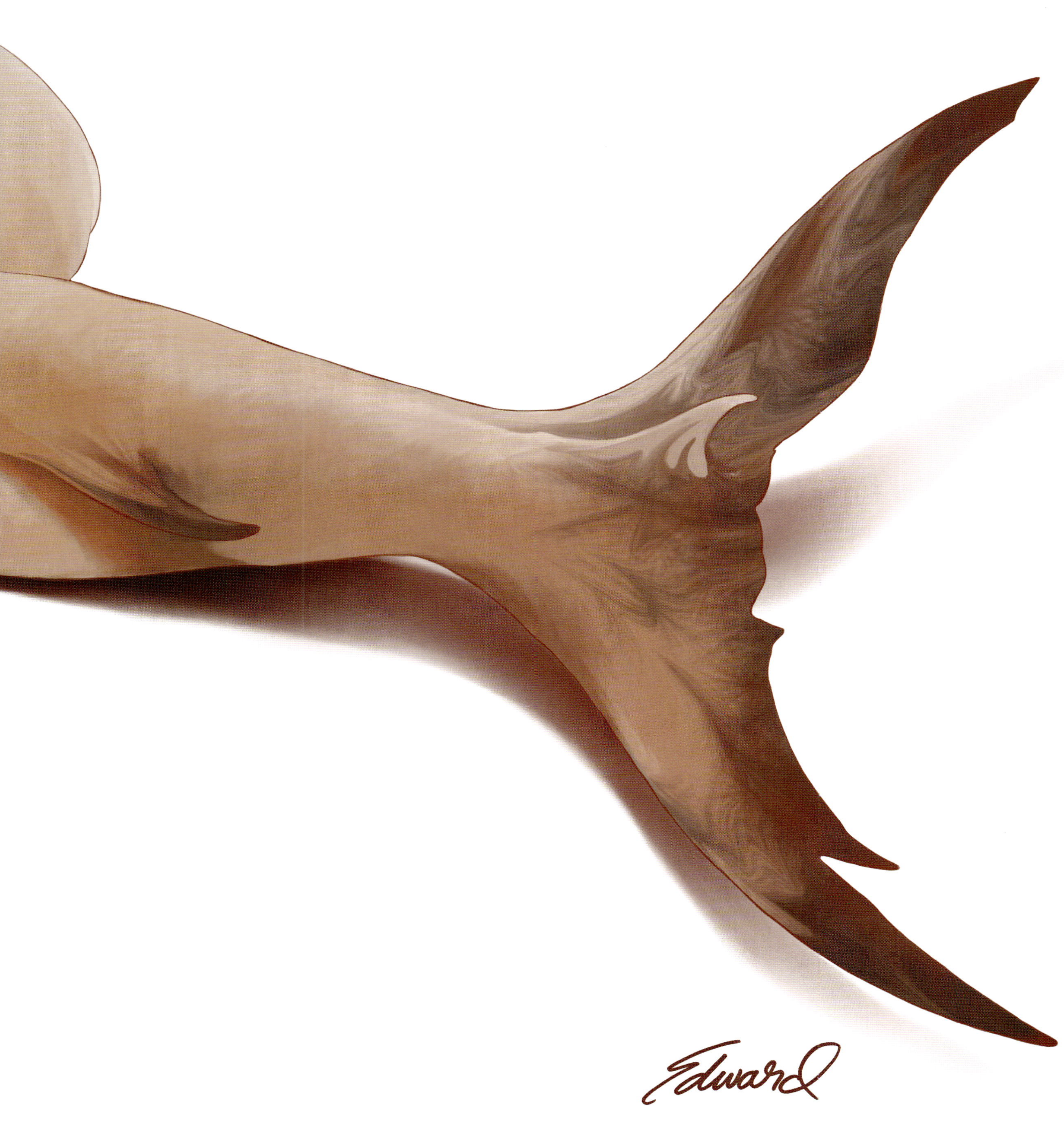

Persephone

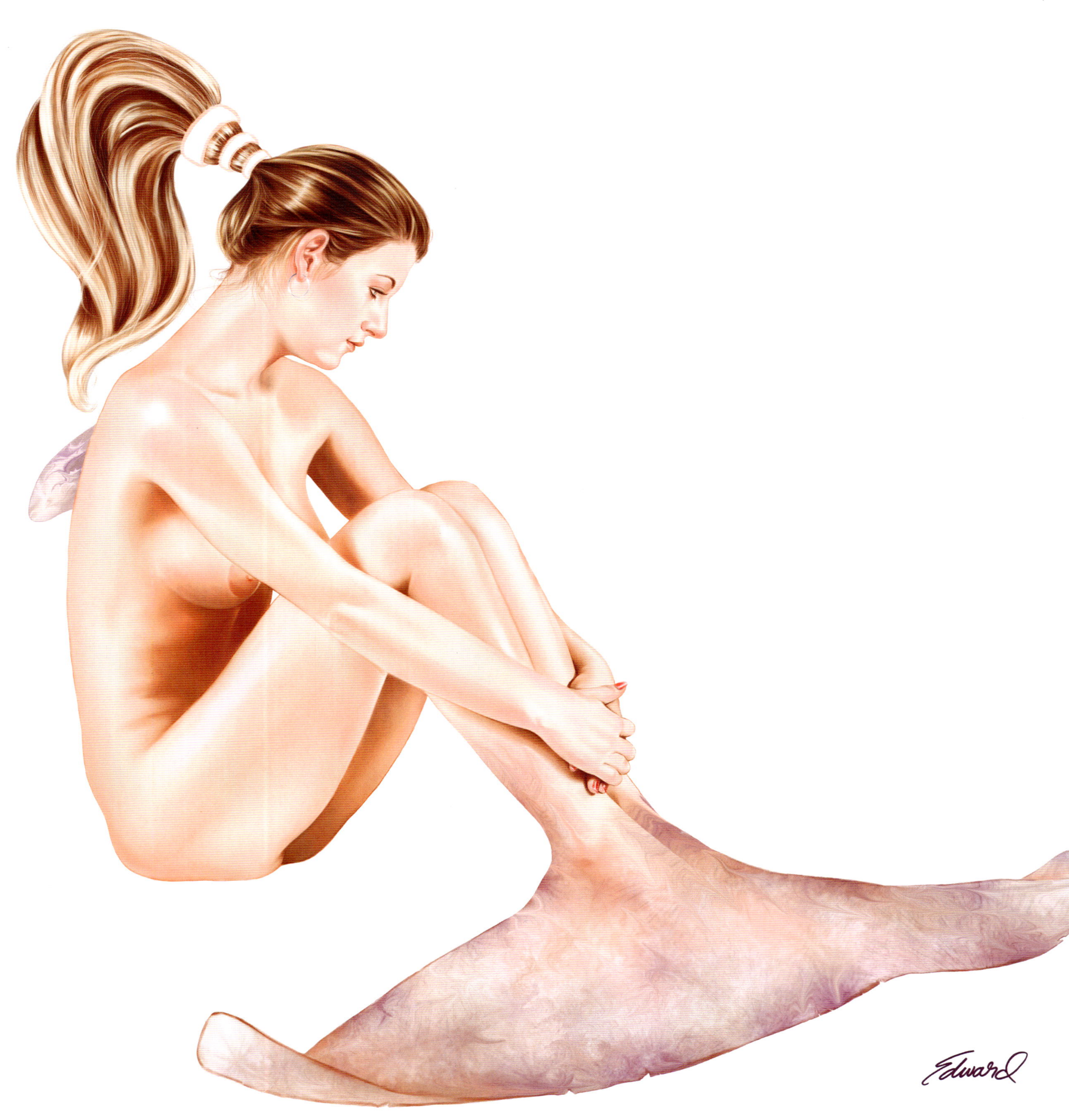

Wax and Wane

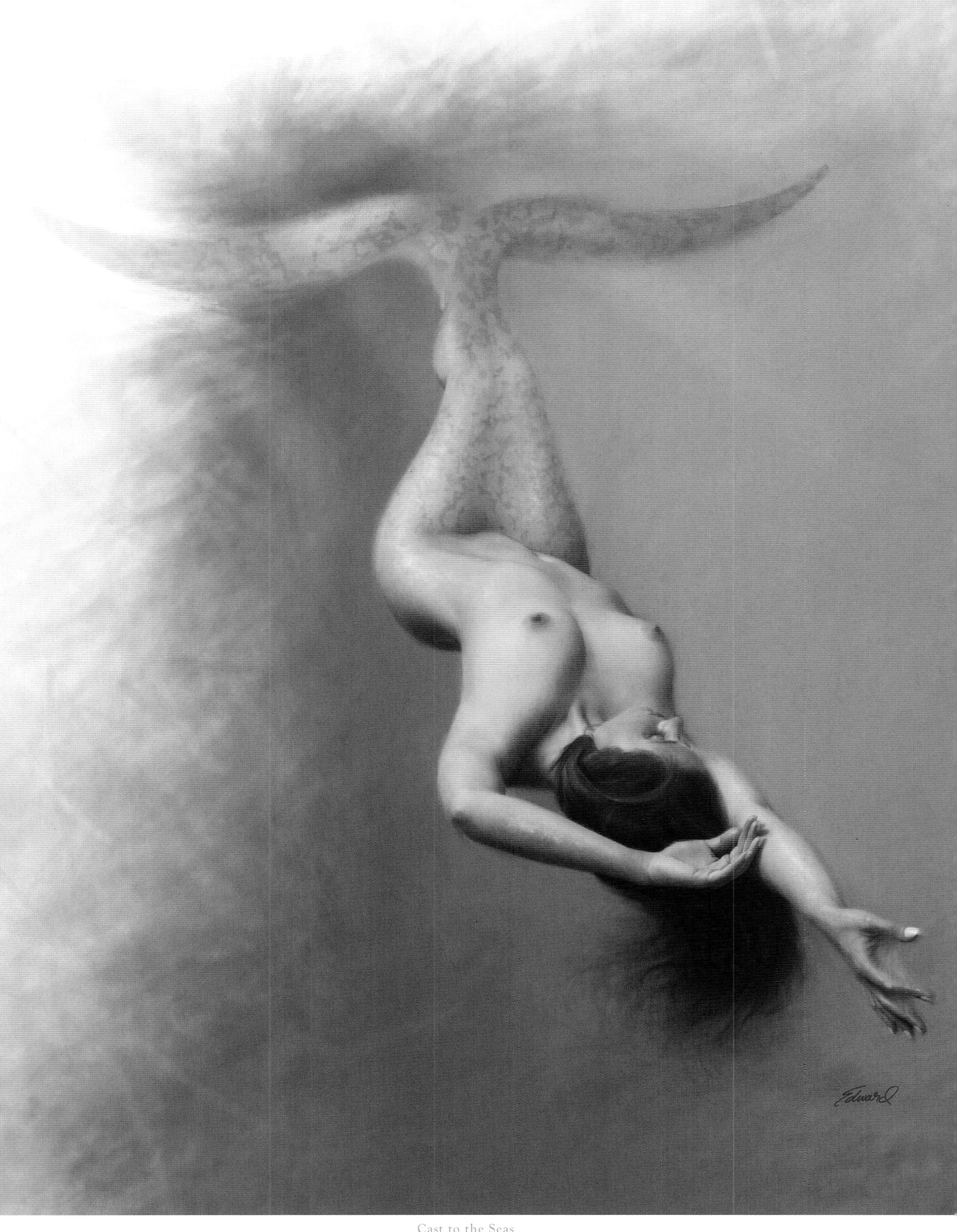

Cast to the Seas

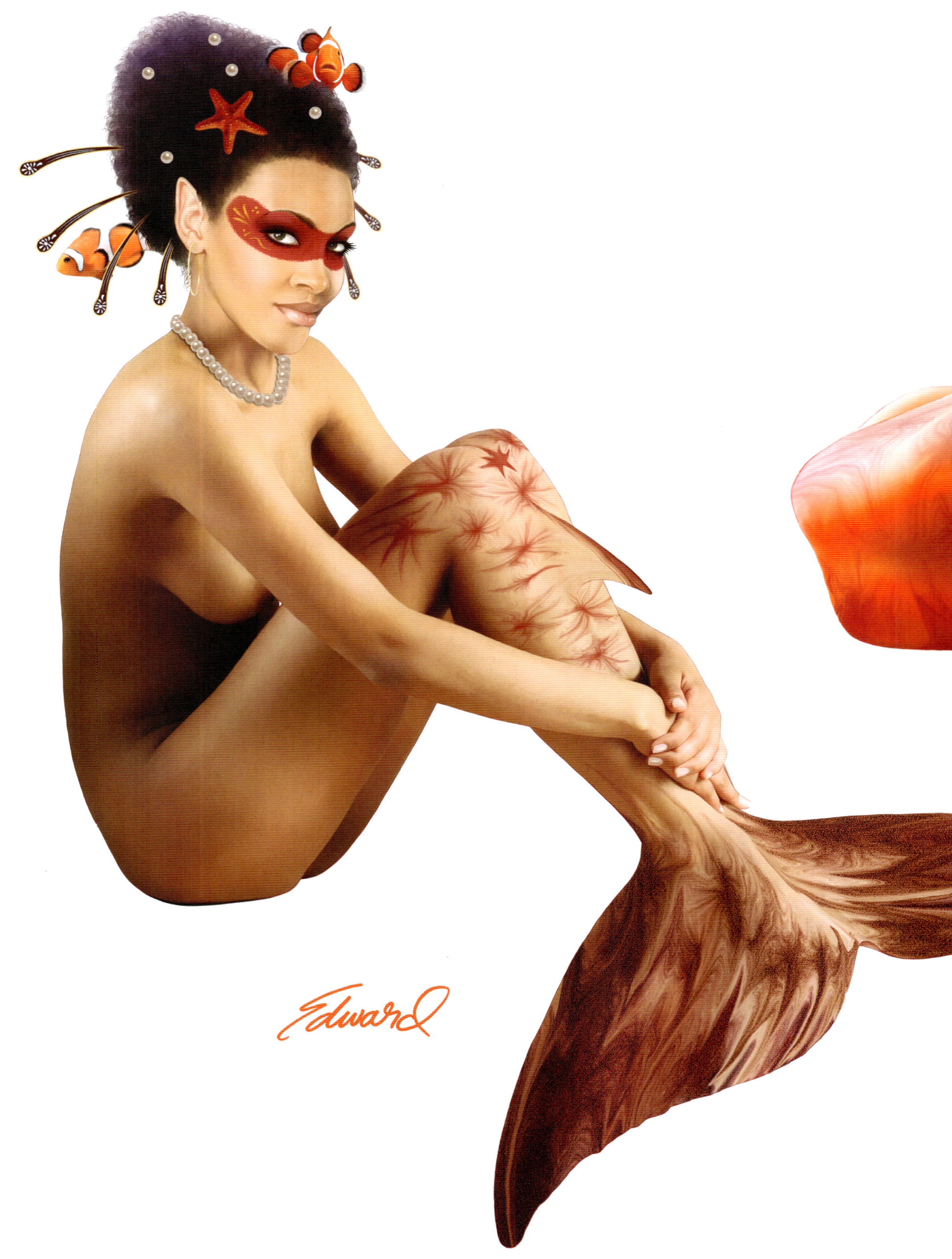

Coral Queen

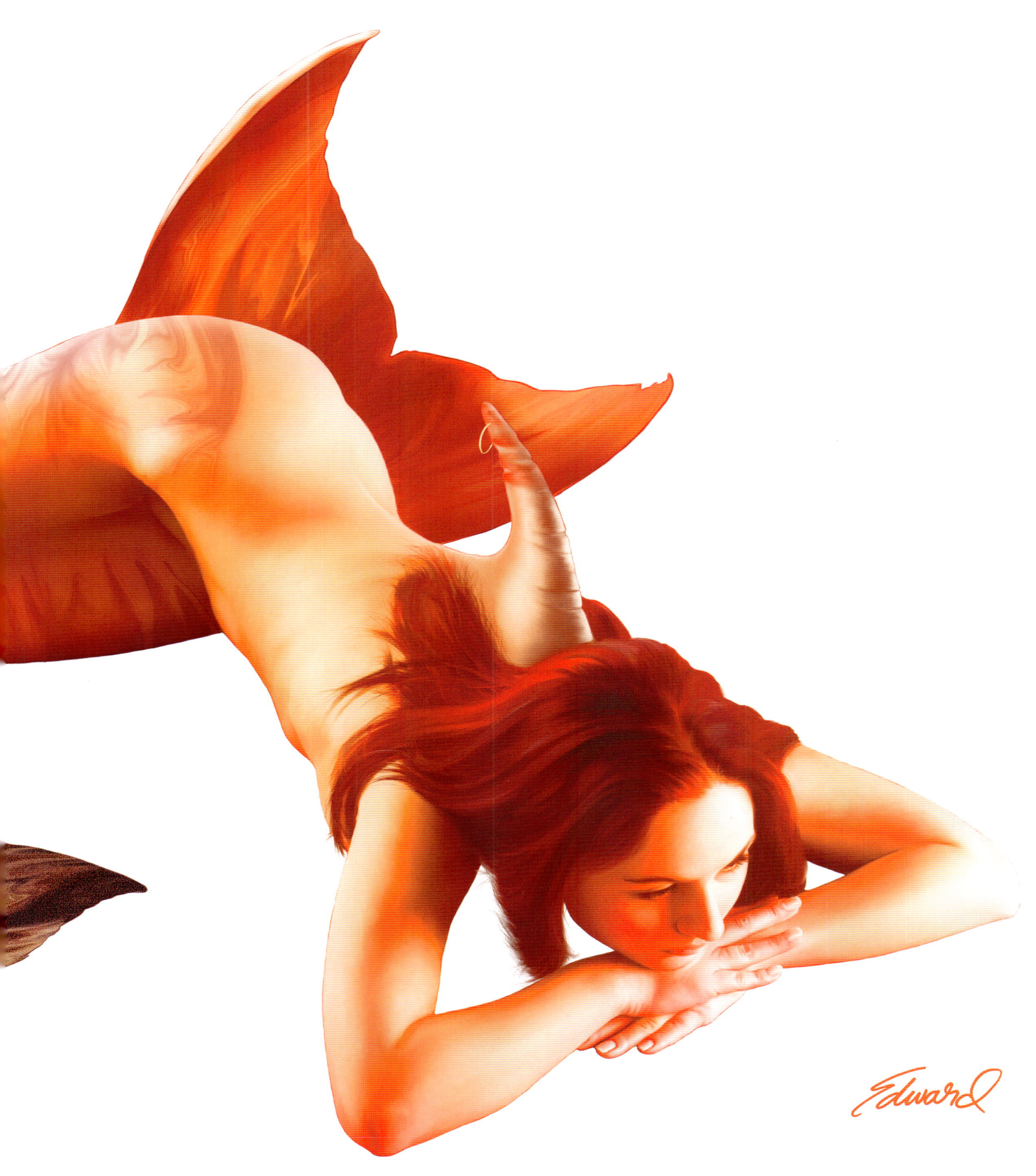

Dazzle

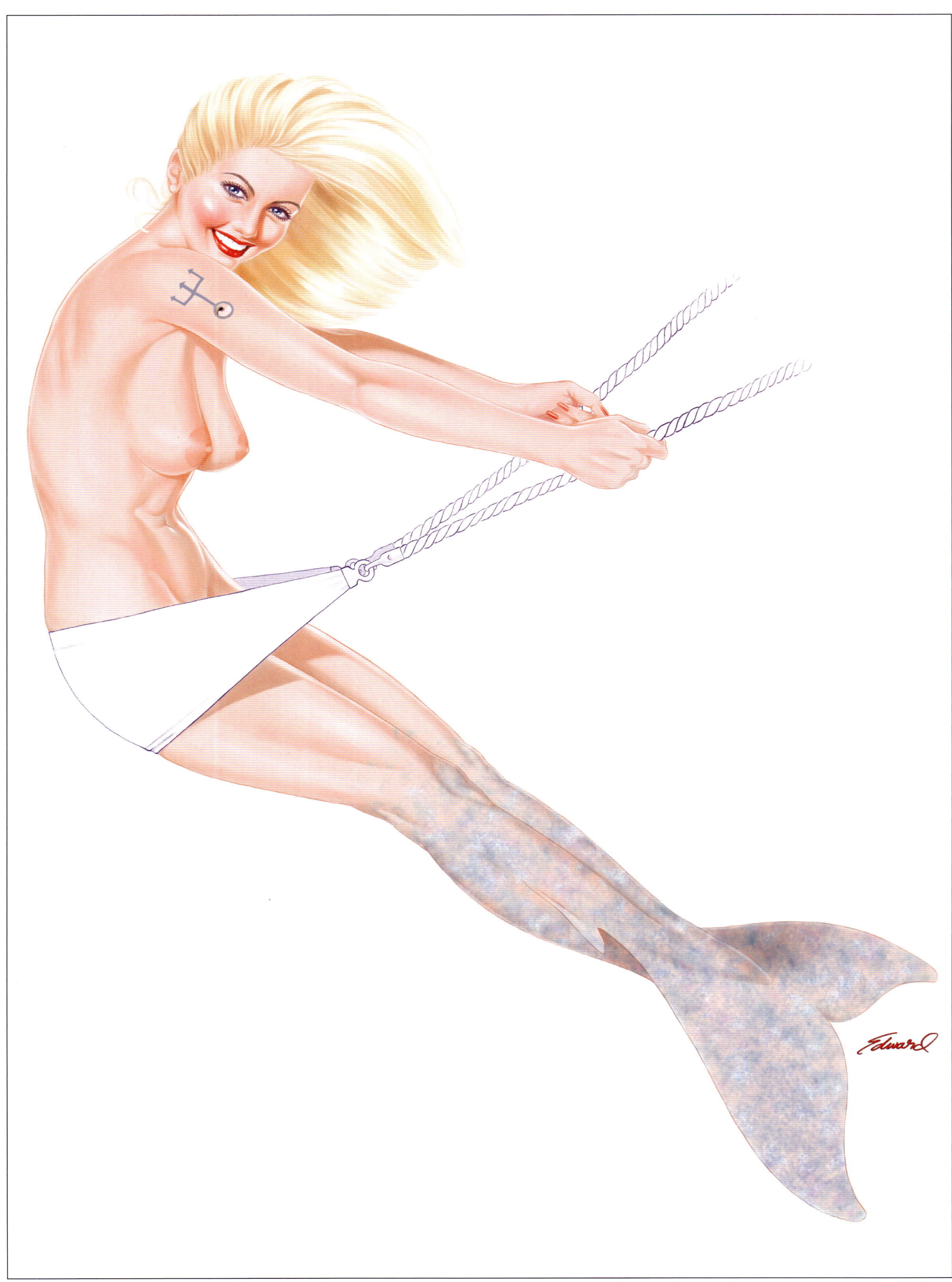

Neptune's Swing

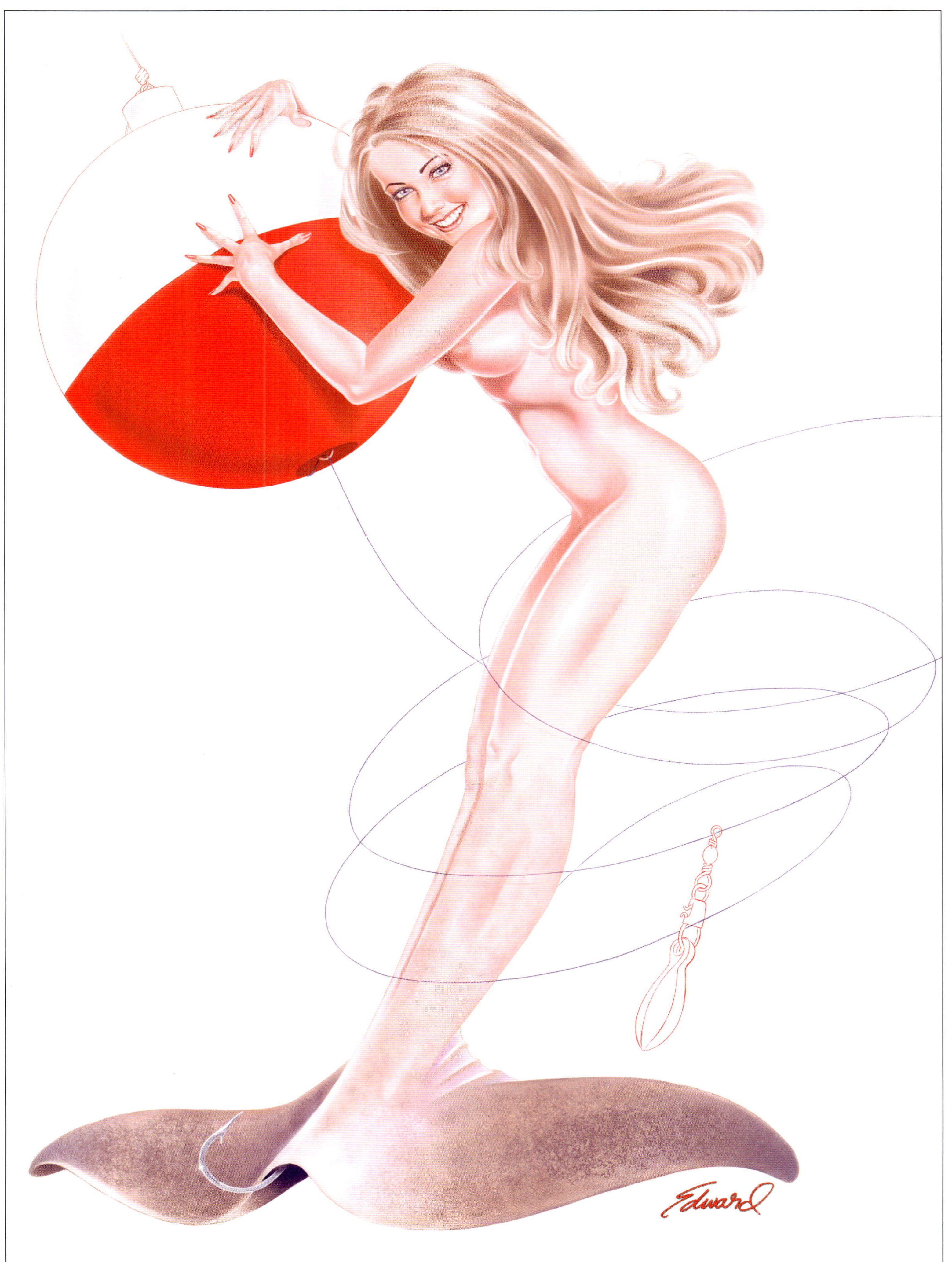

Catch of the Day

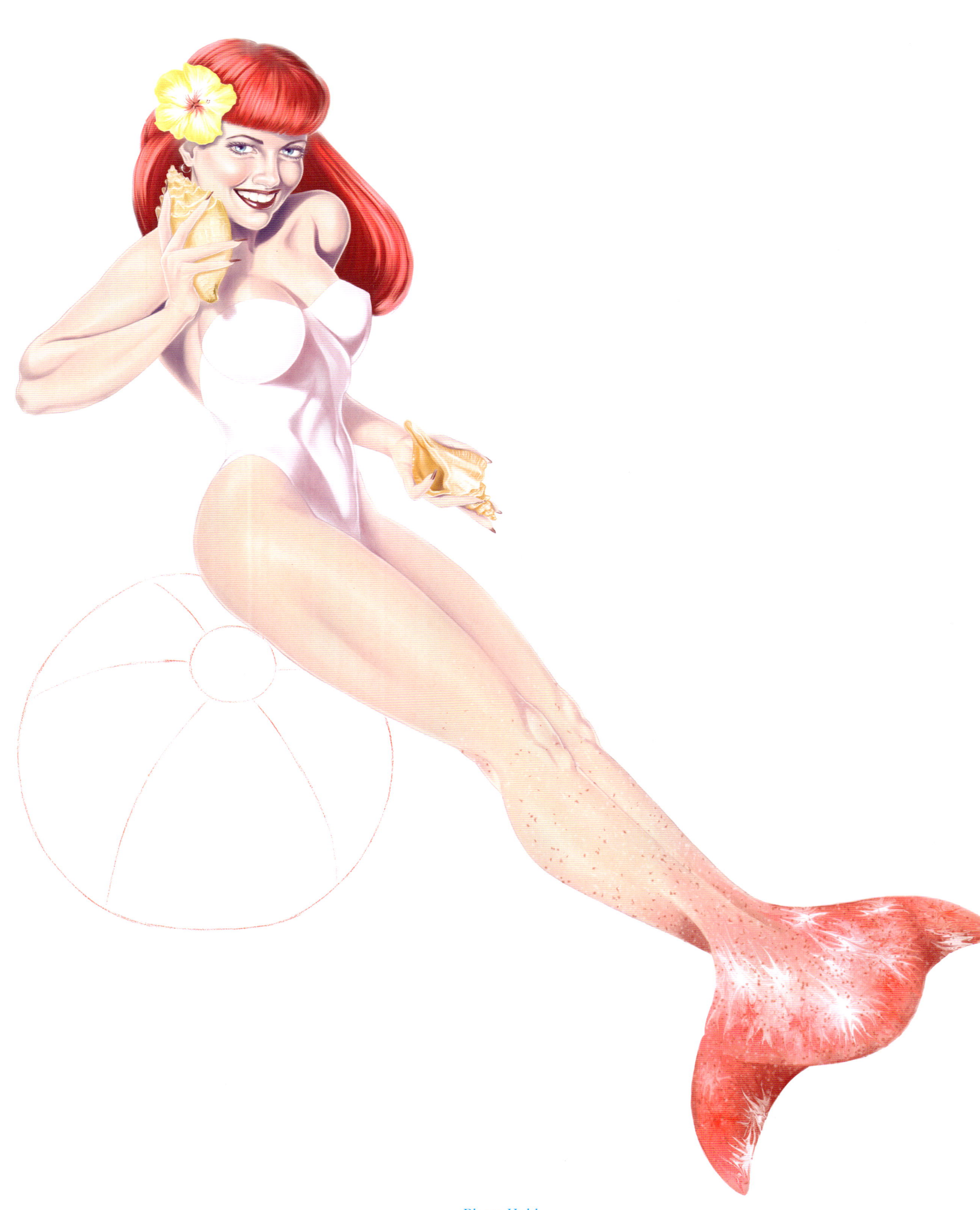

Please Hold

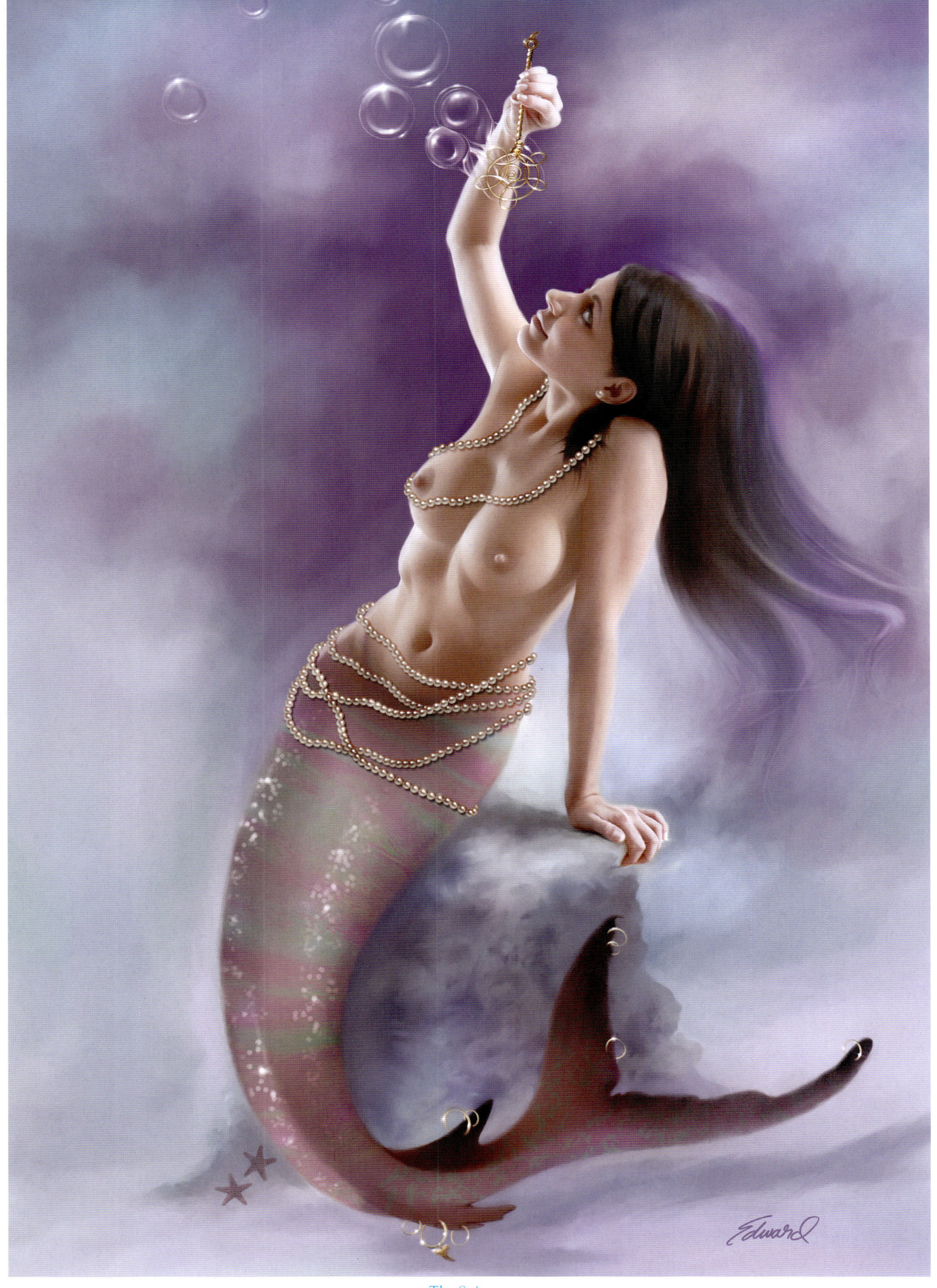

The Spinner

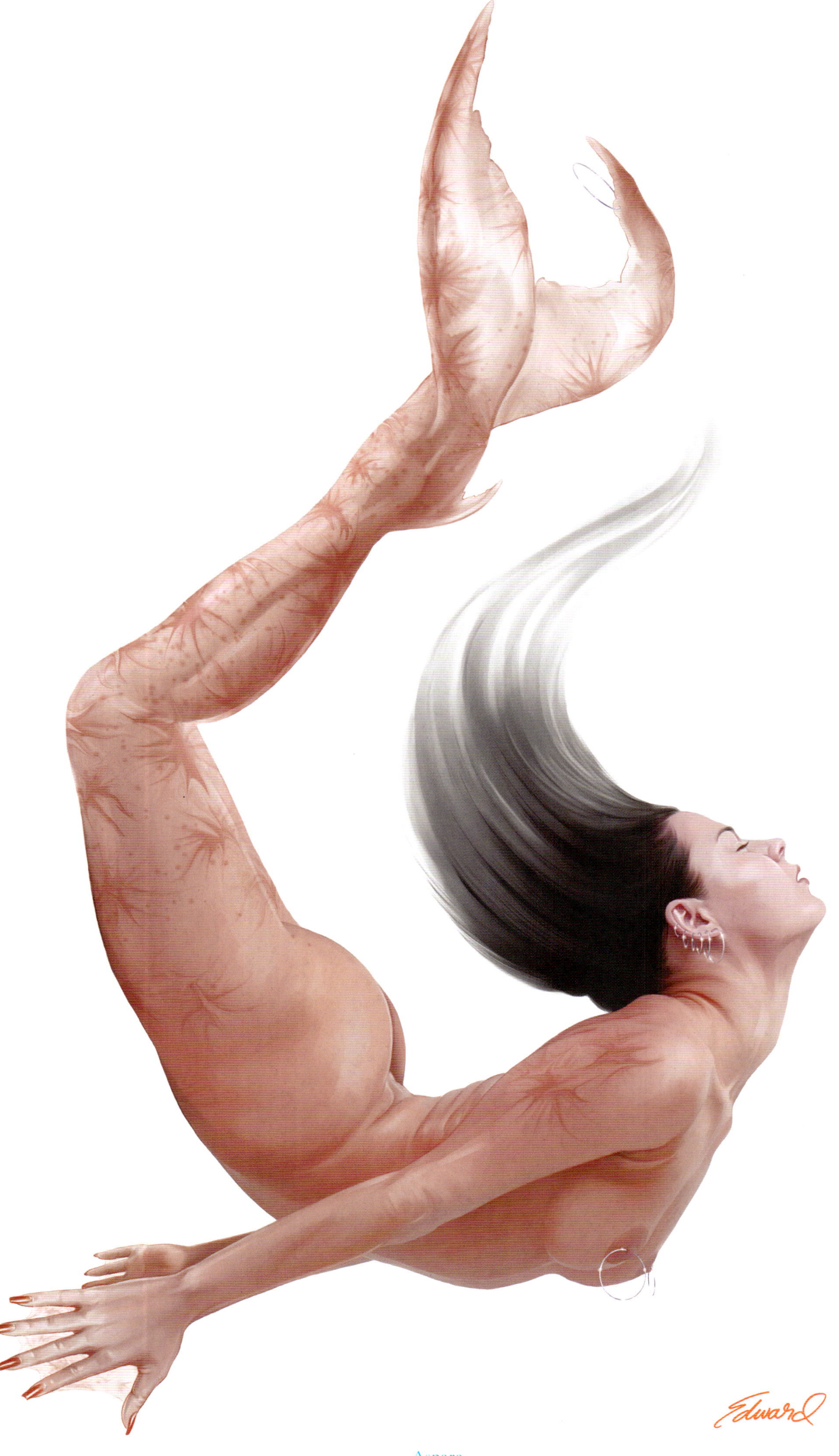

Aspara

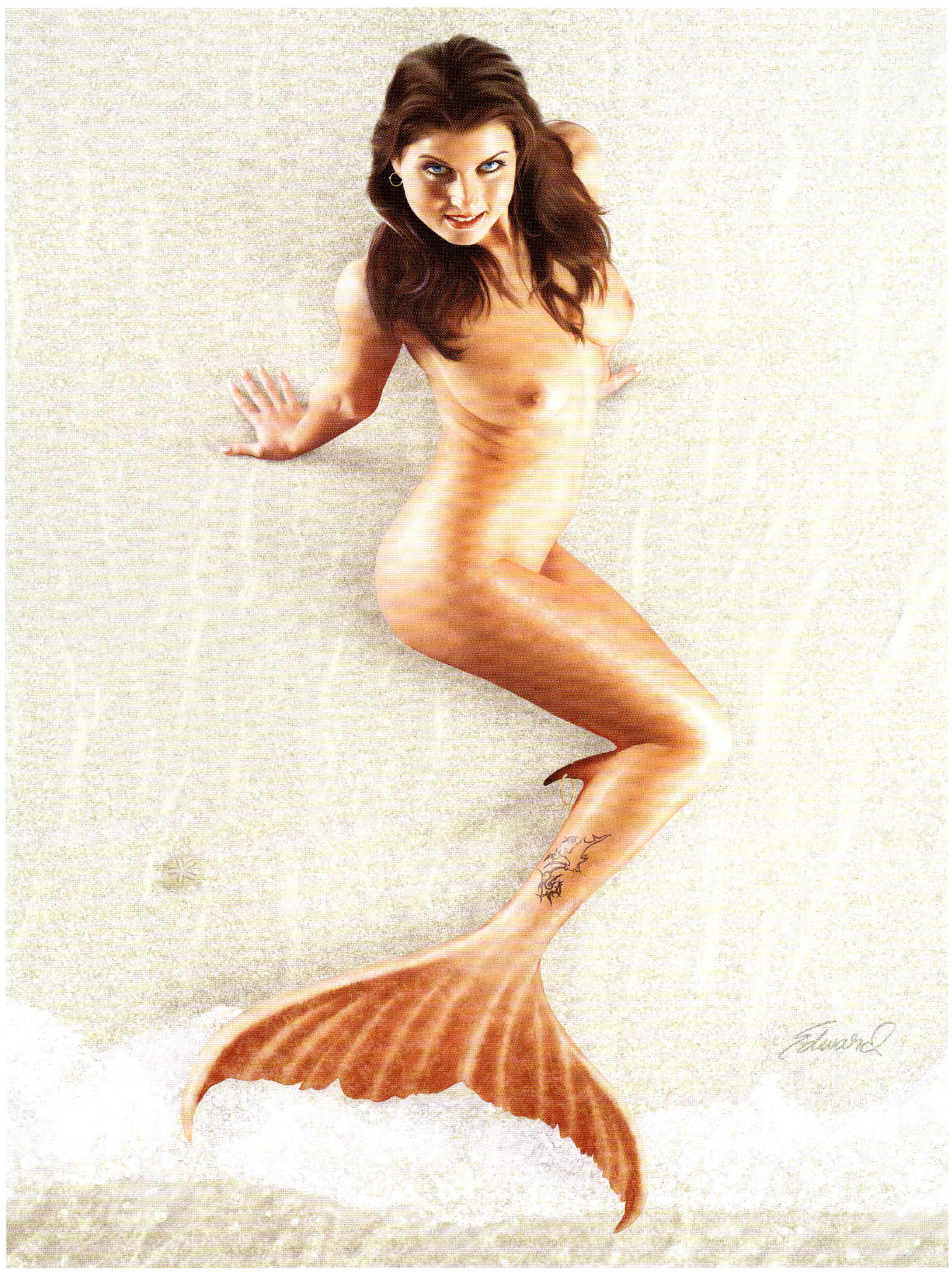

She Sells Sea Shells

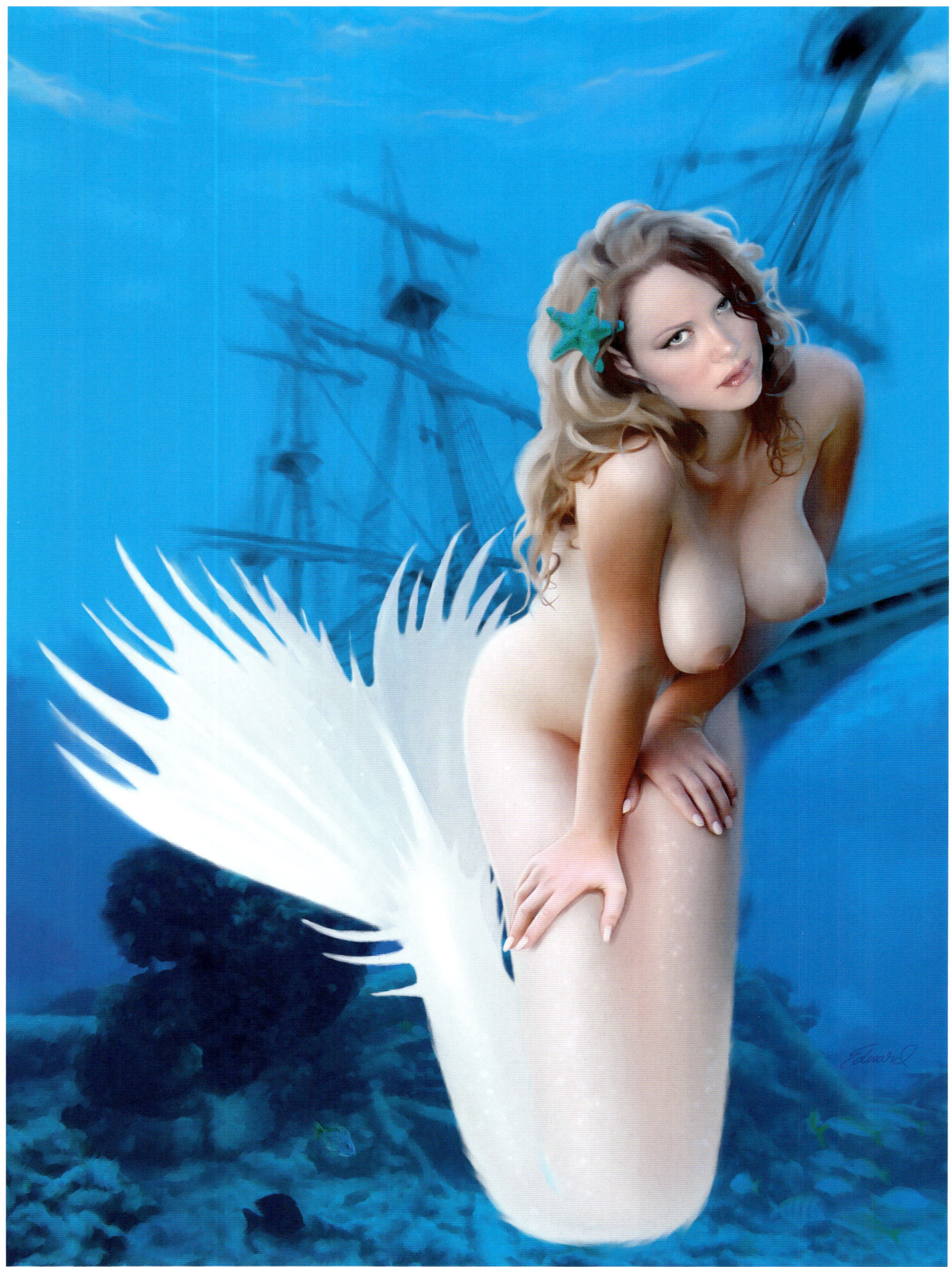

Shipwrecker

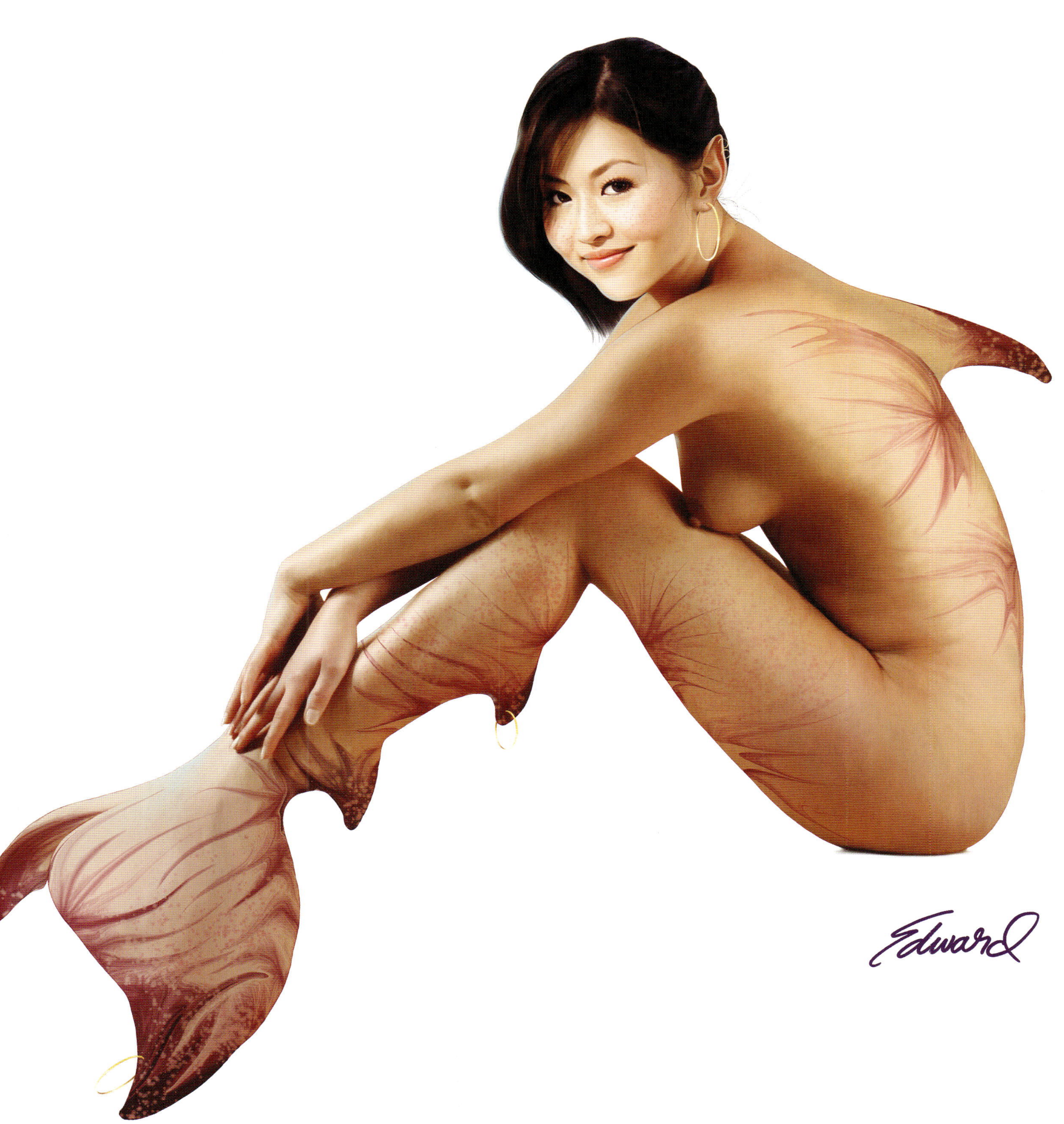

Sobakasu

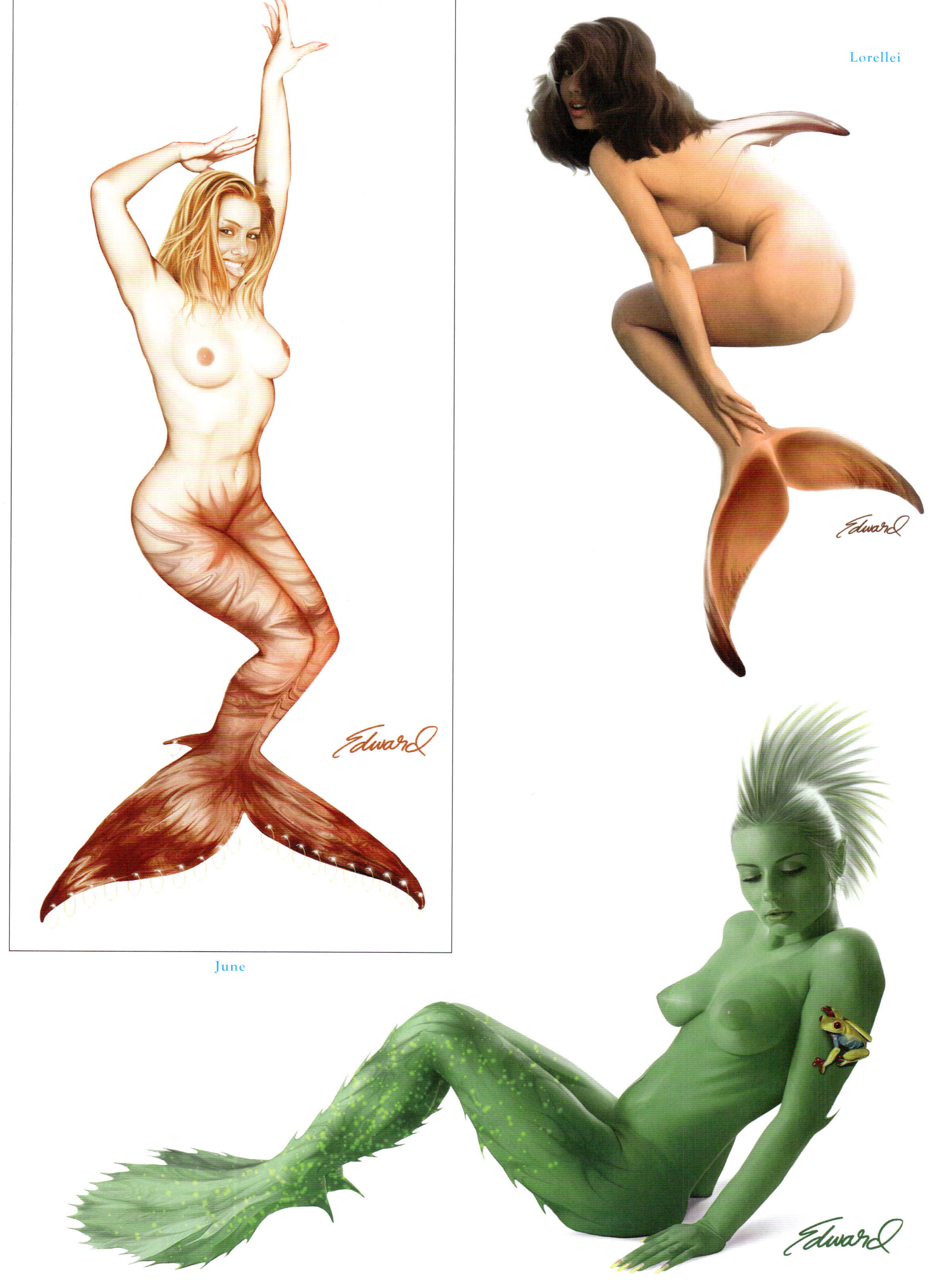

Lorellei

June

Creaturette

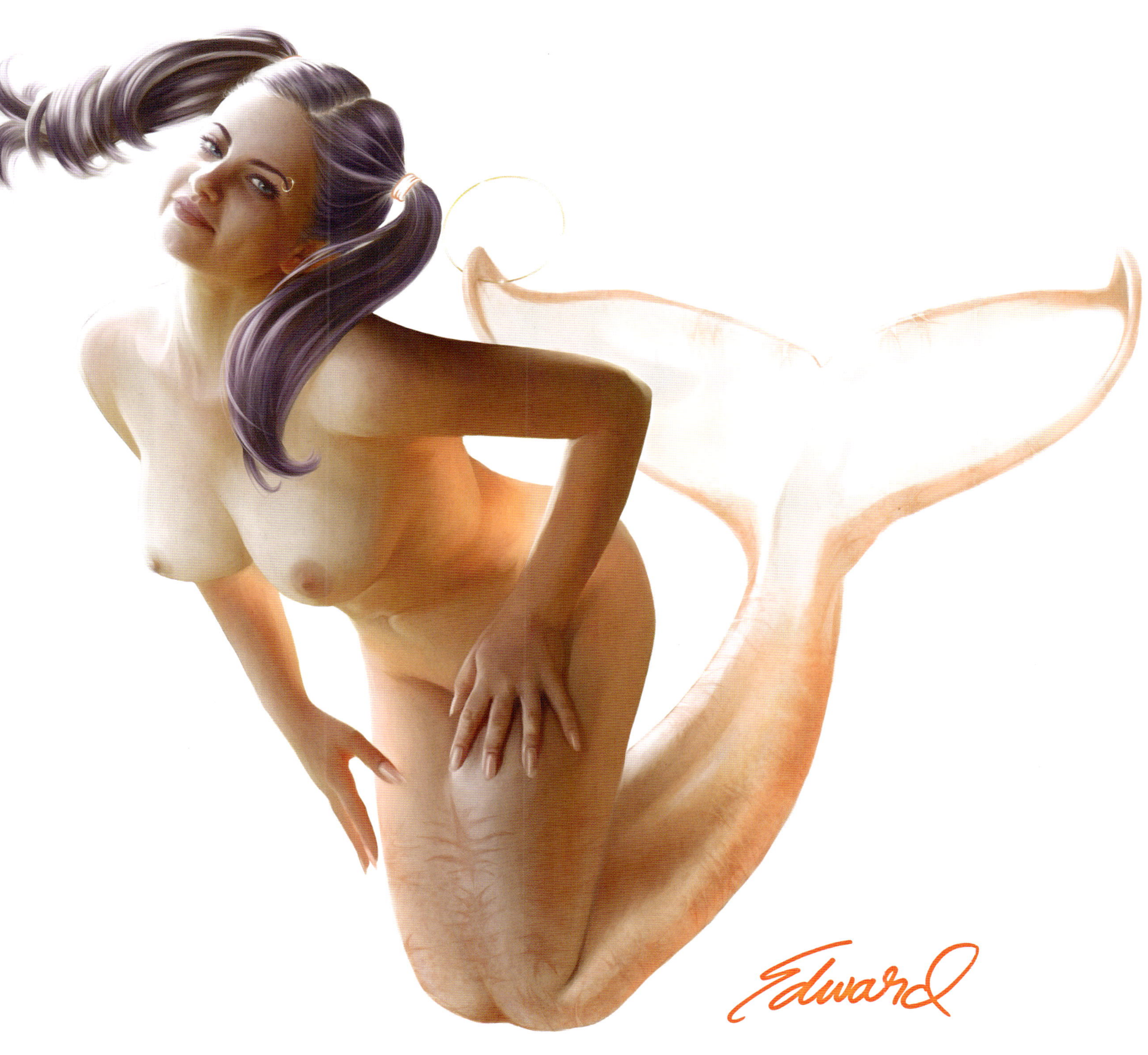

Whirlygigs

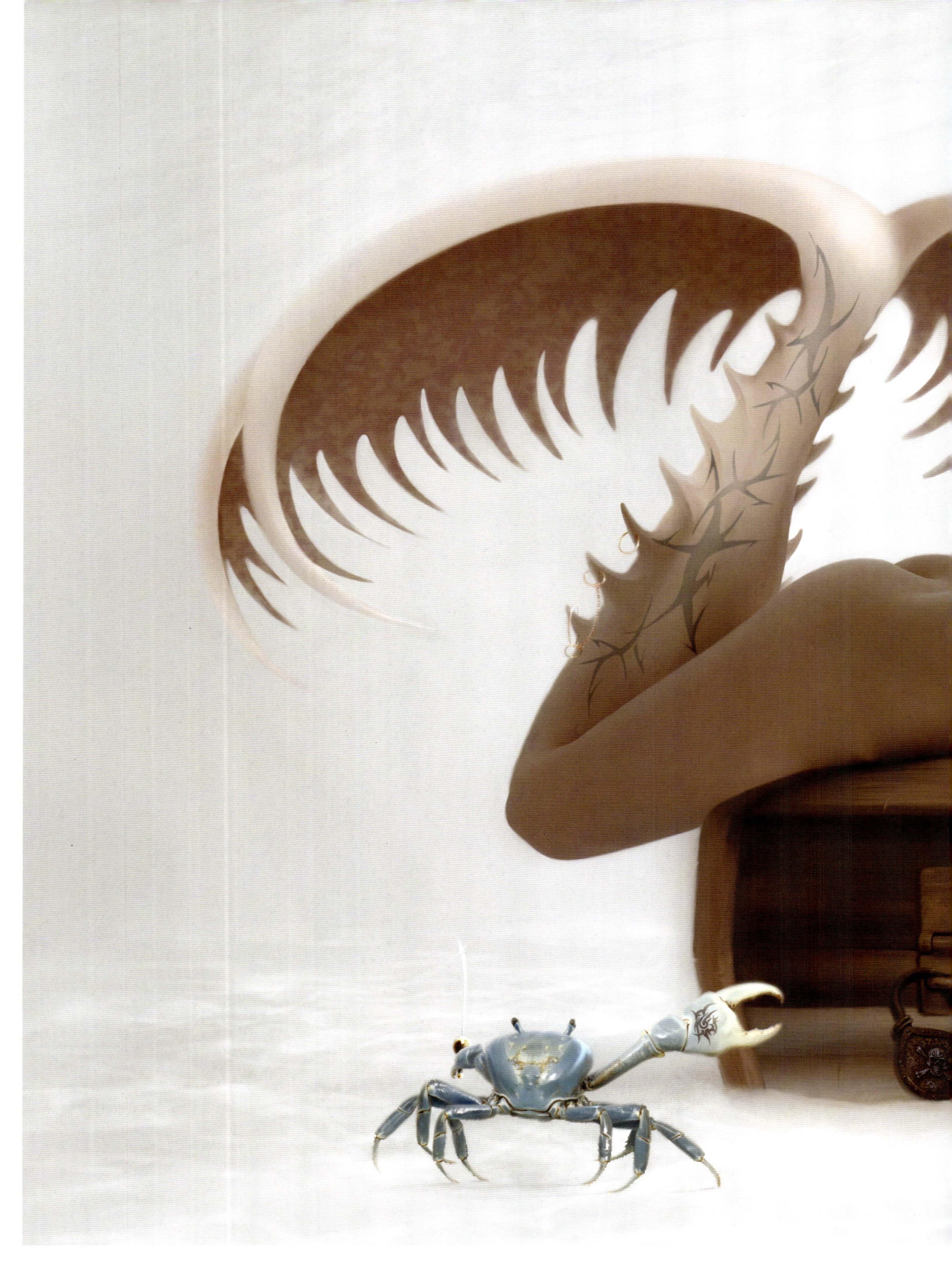

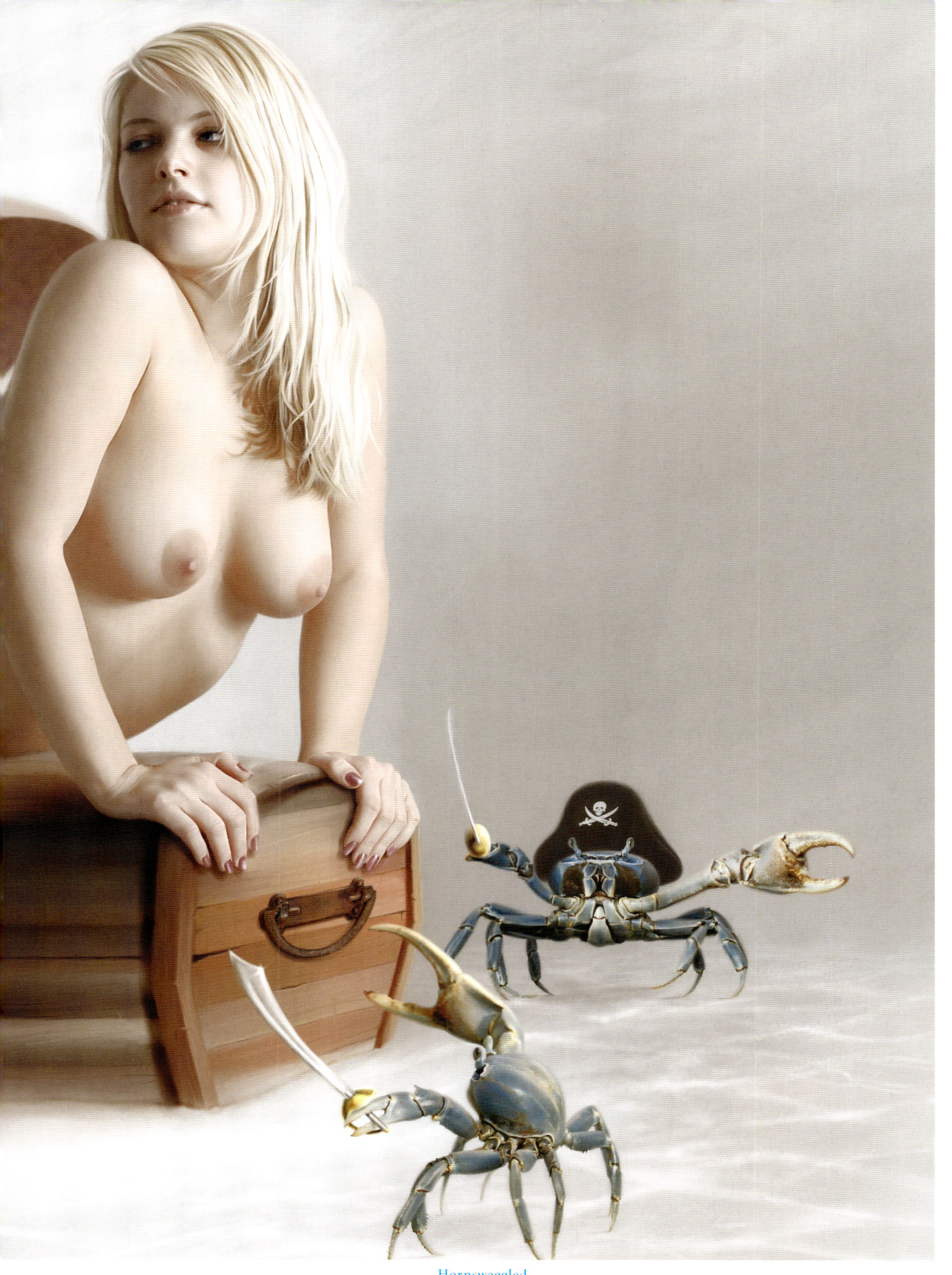

Hornswaggled

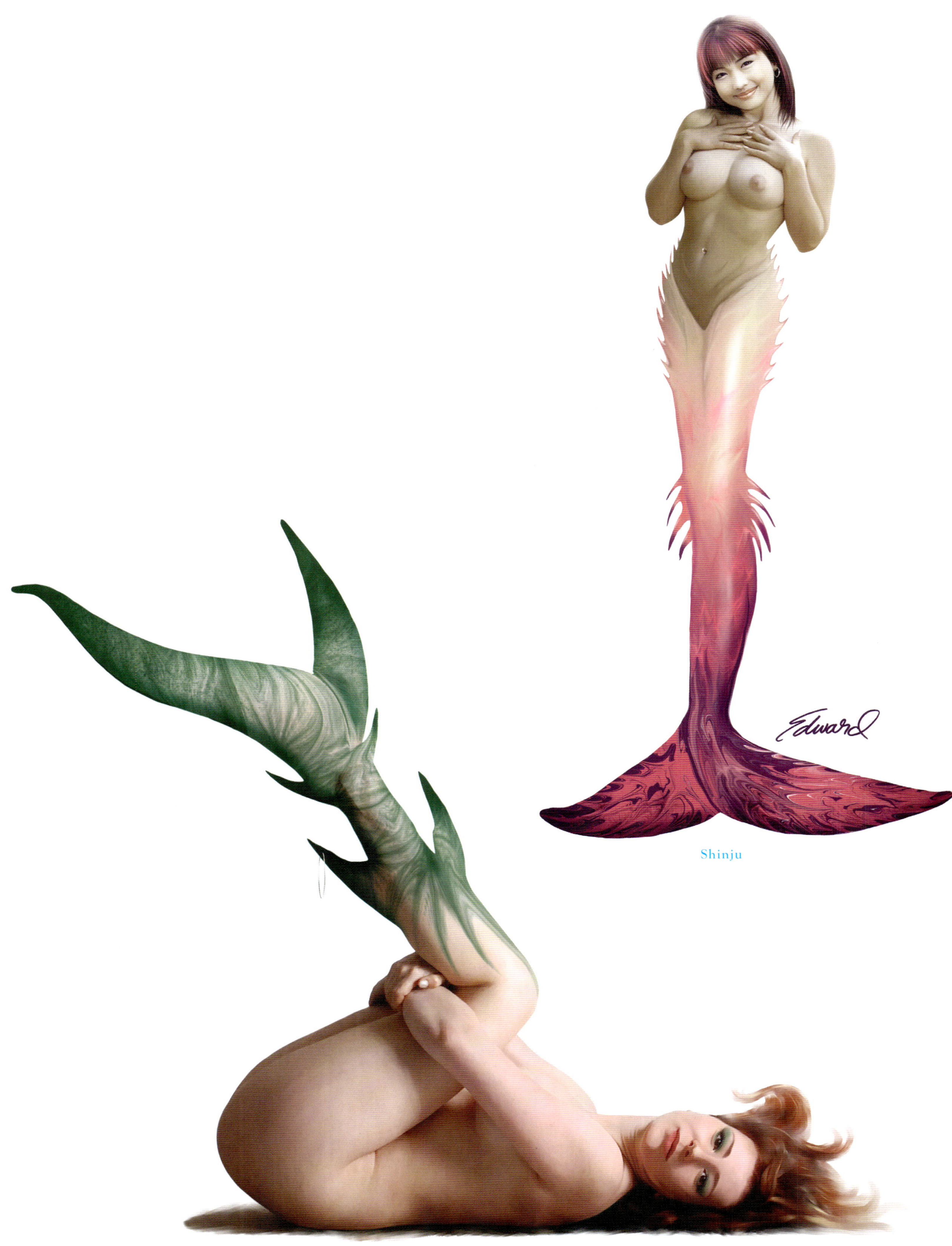

Shinju

Tropical Depression

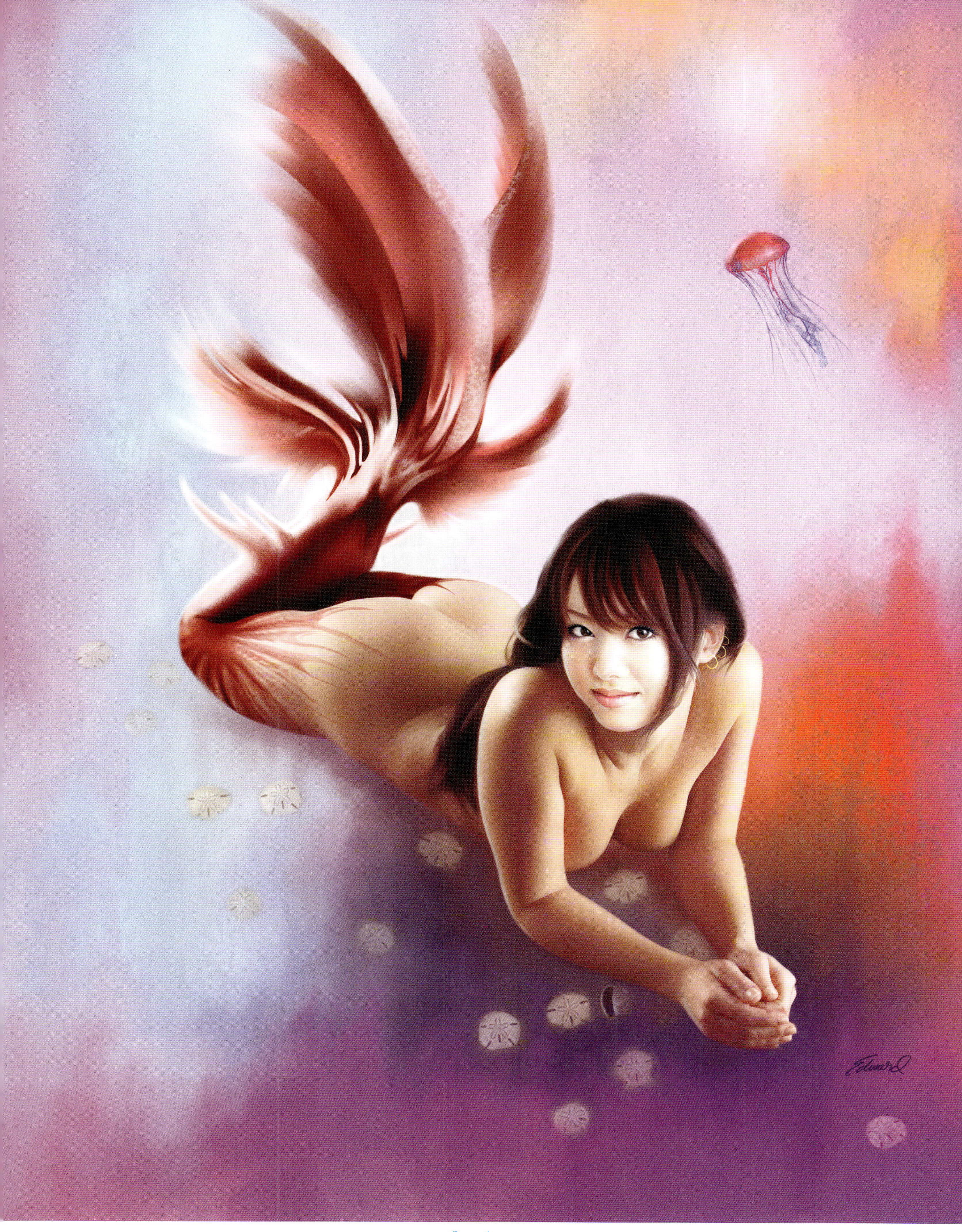

Sayuri

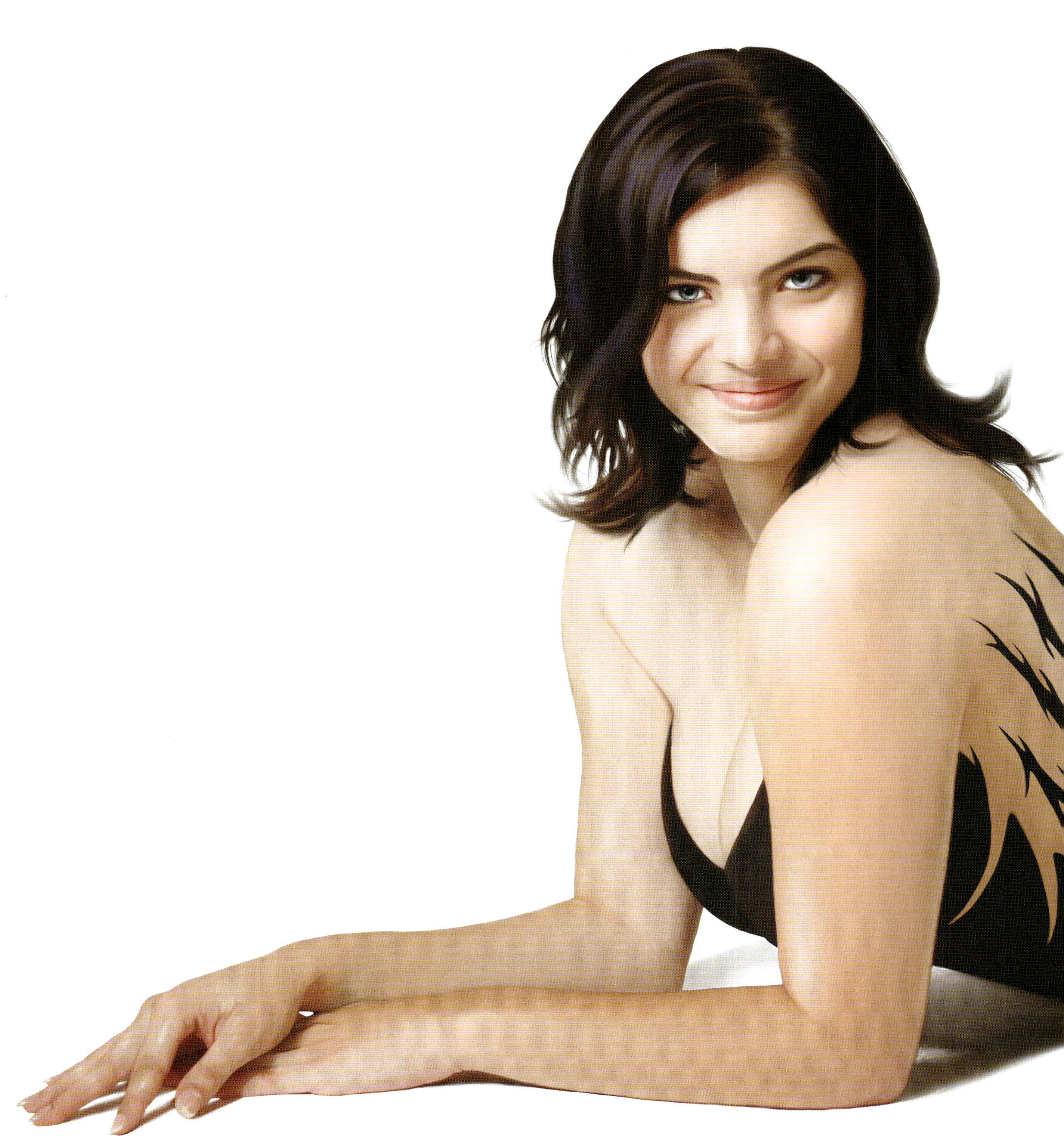

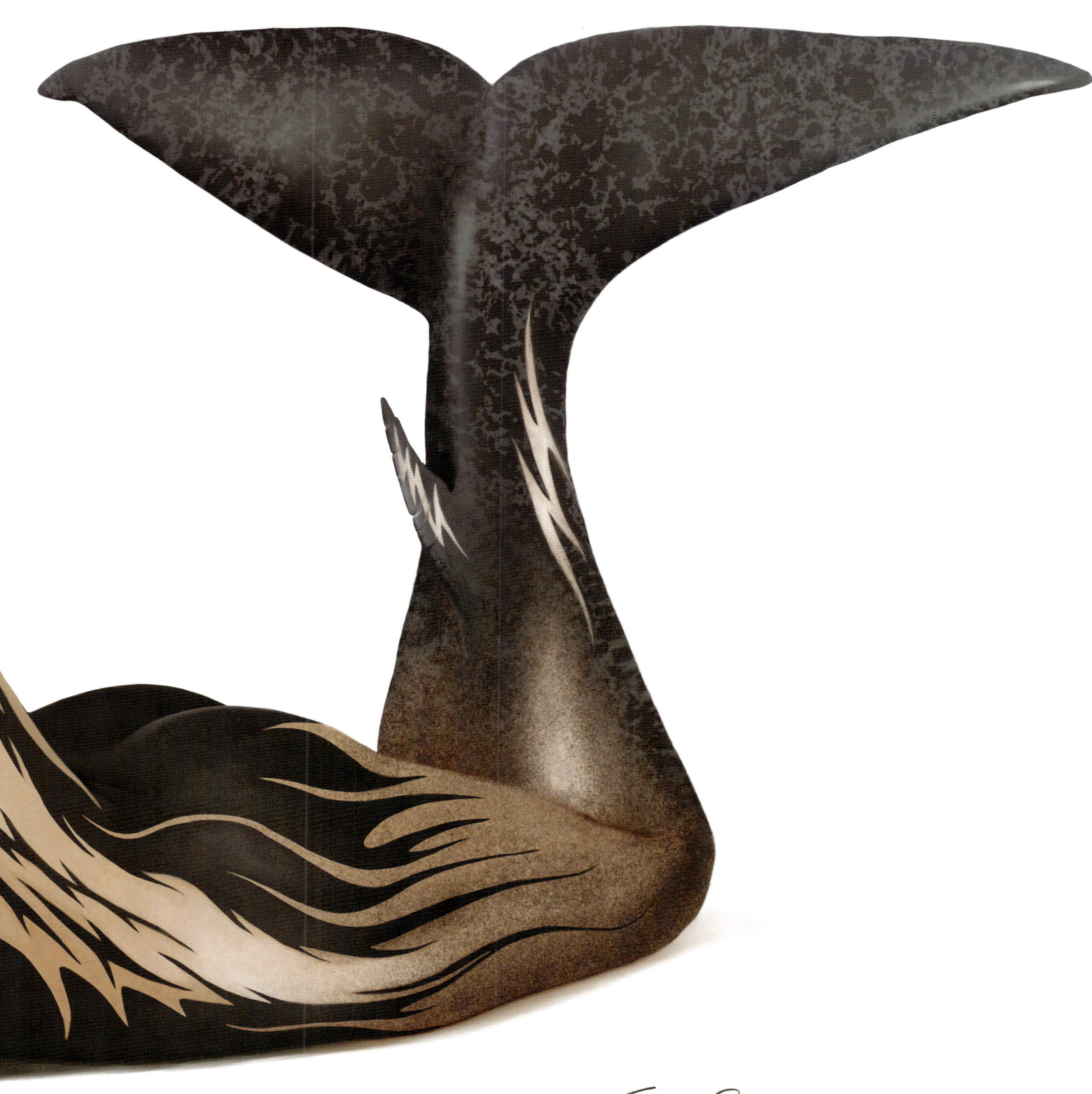

Edward

Riptide

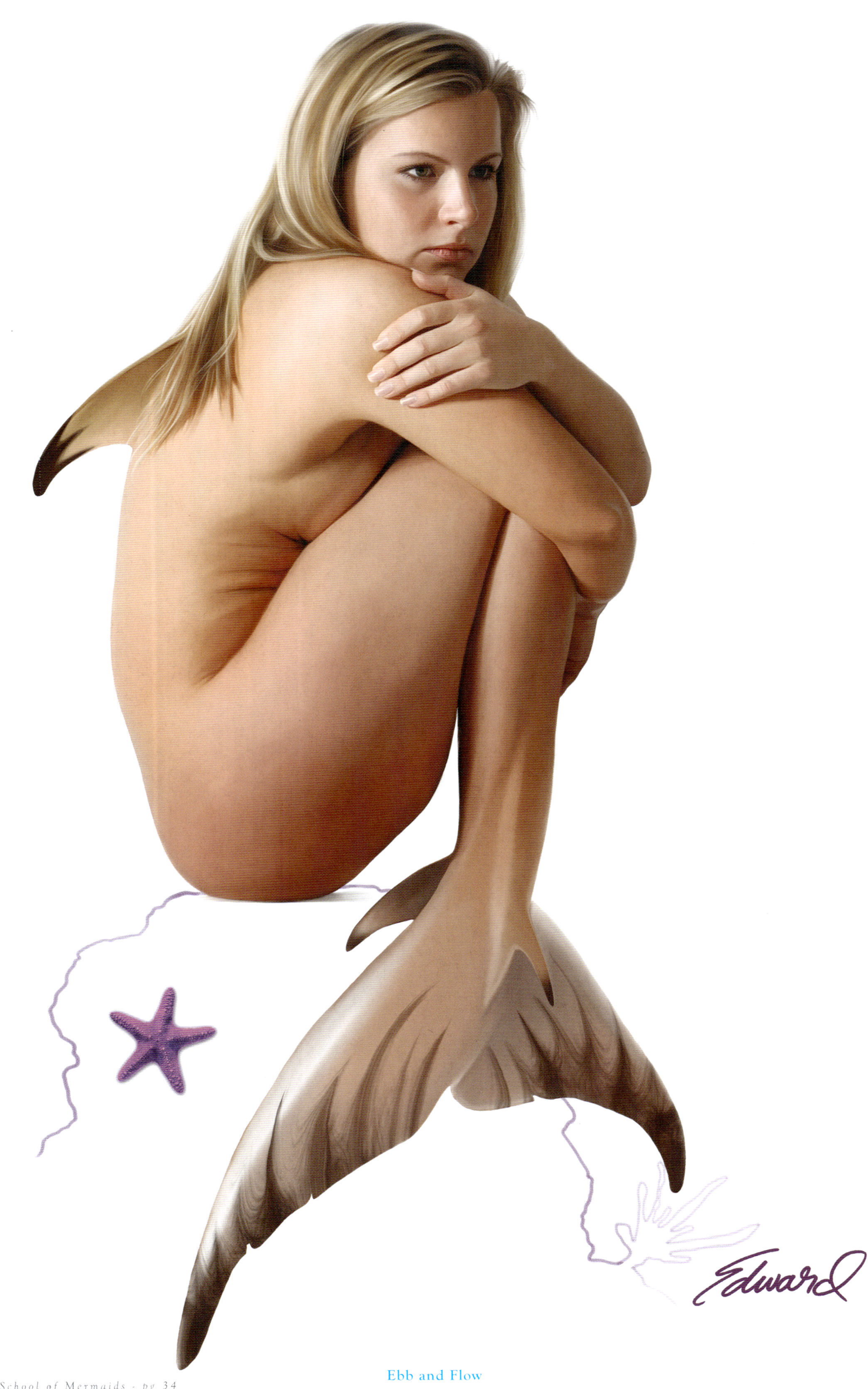

Ebb and Flow

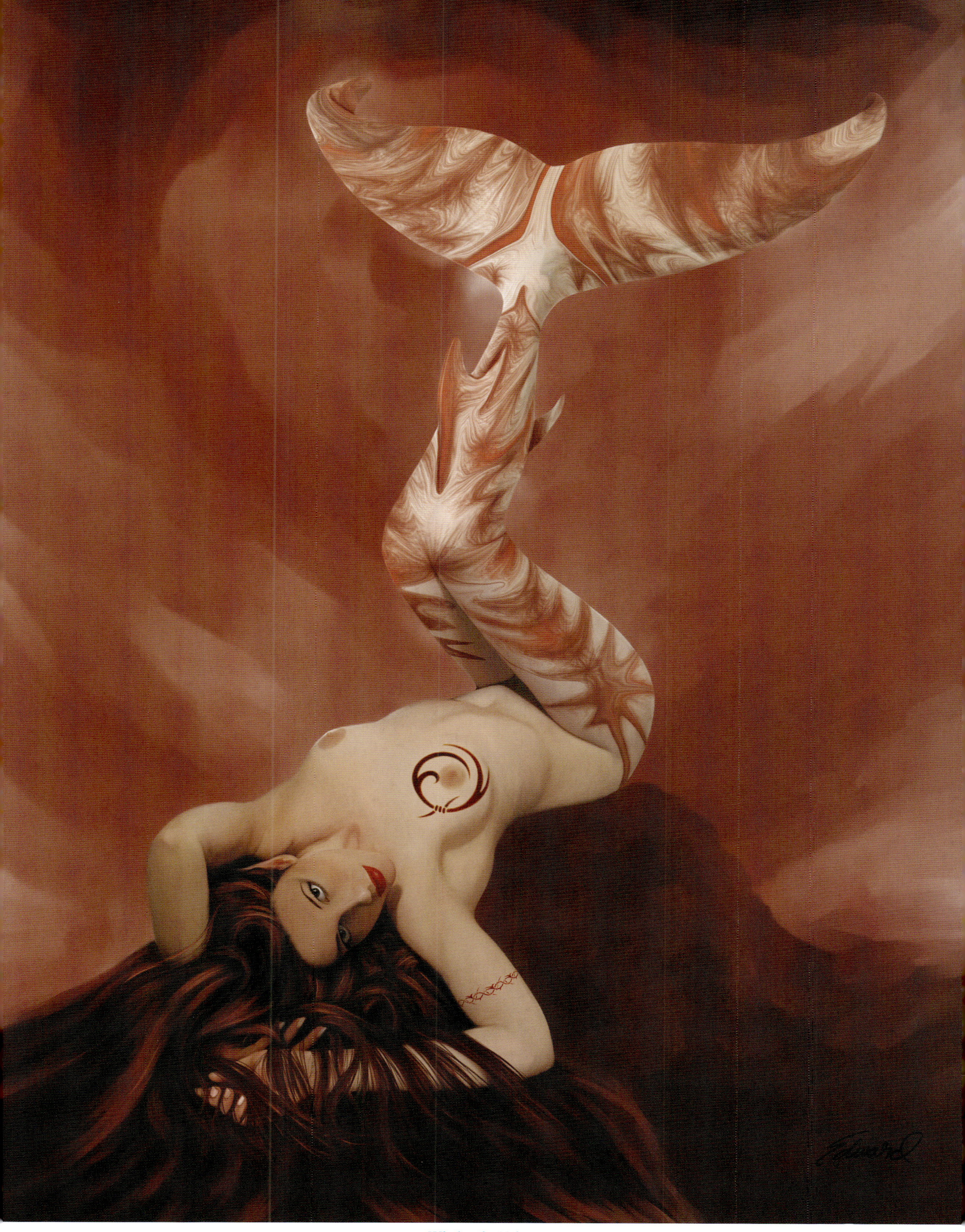

Whale of a Tale

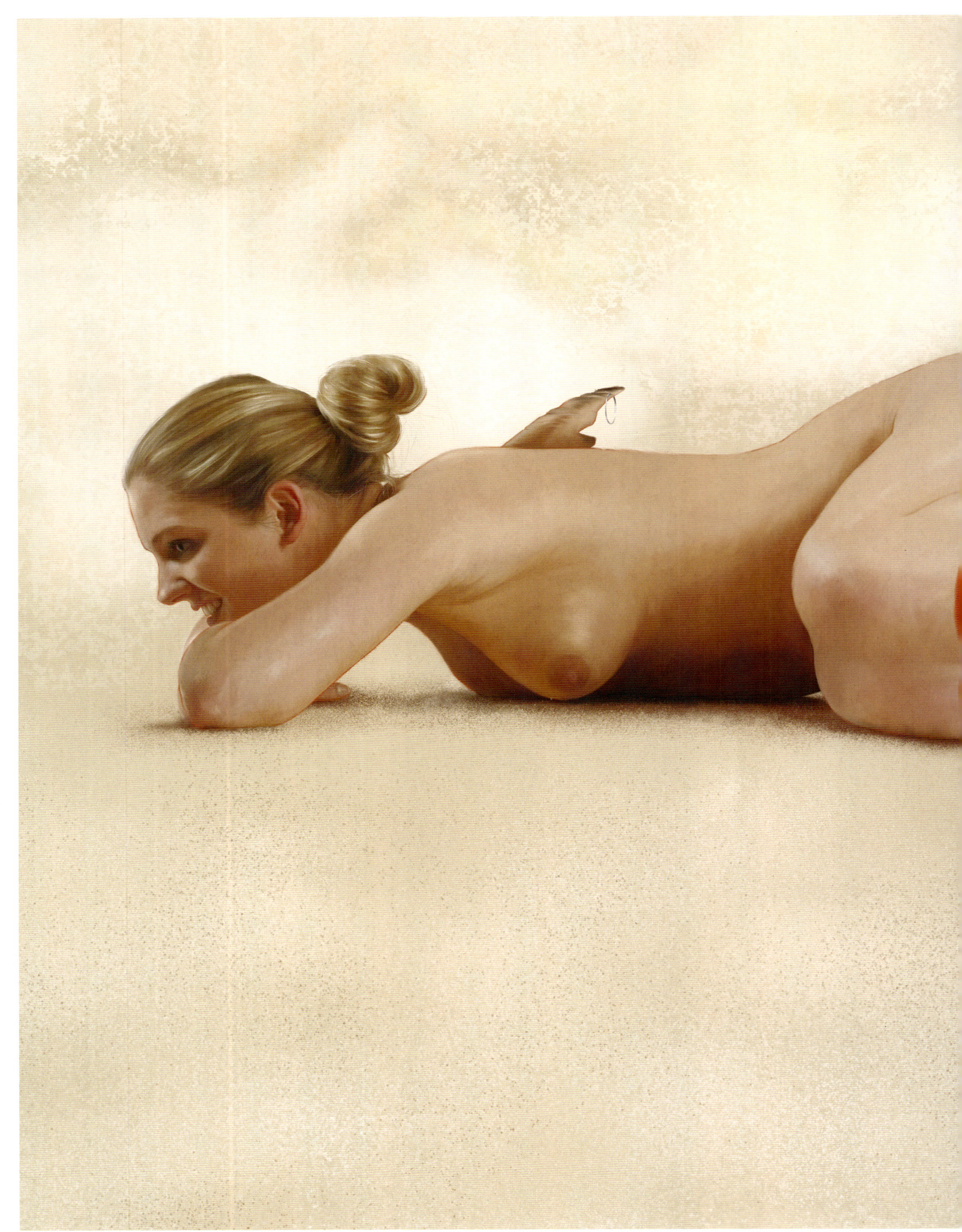

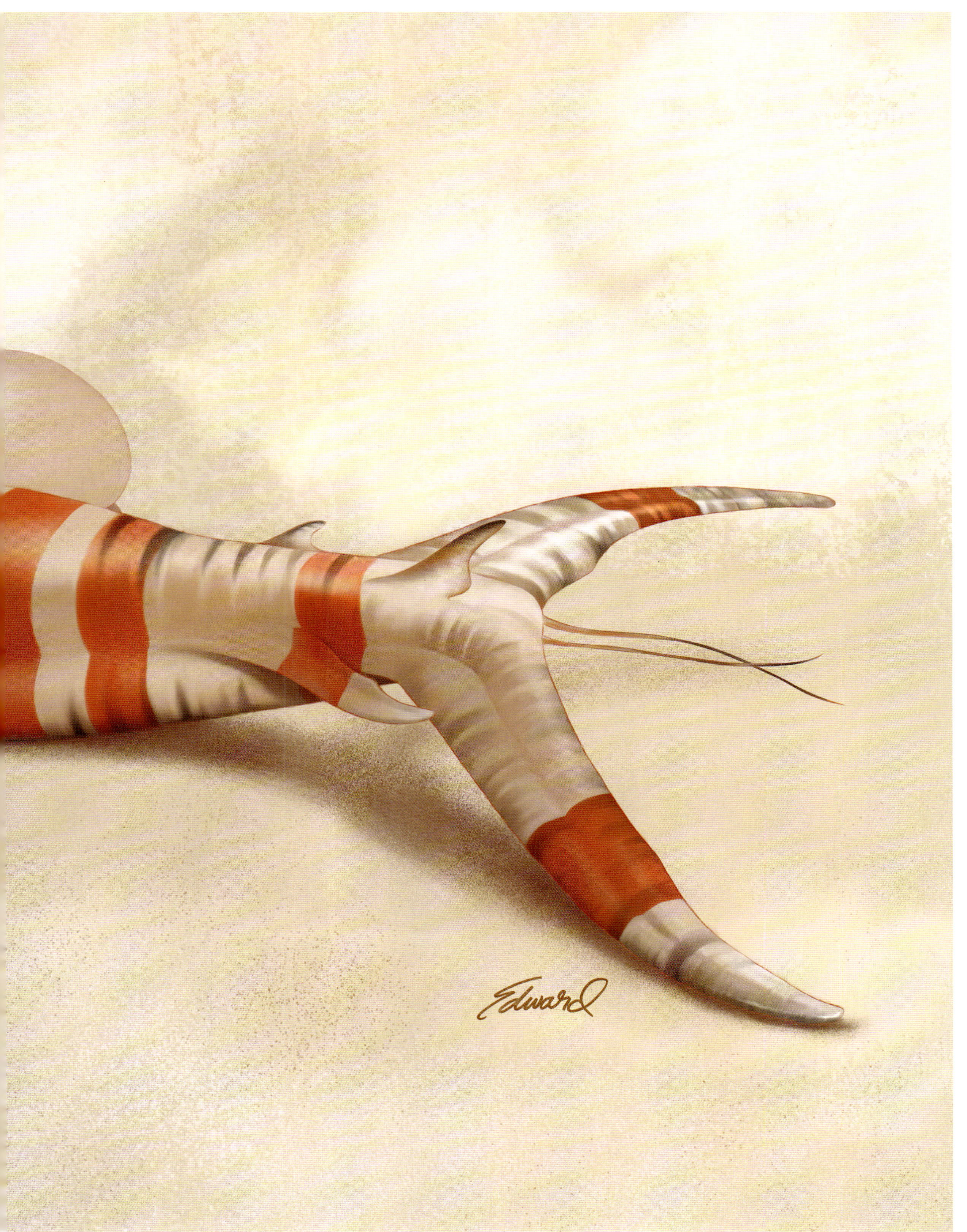

Daydream

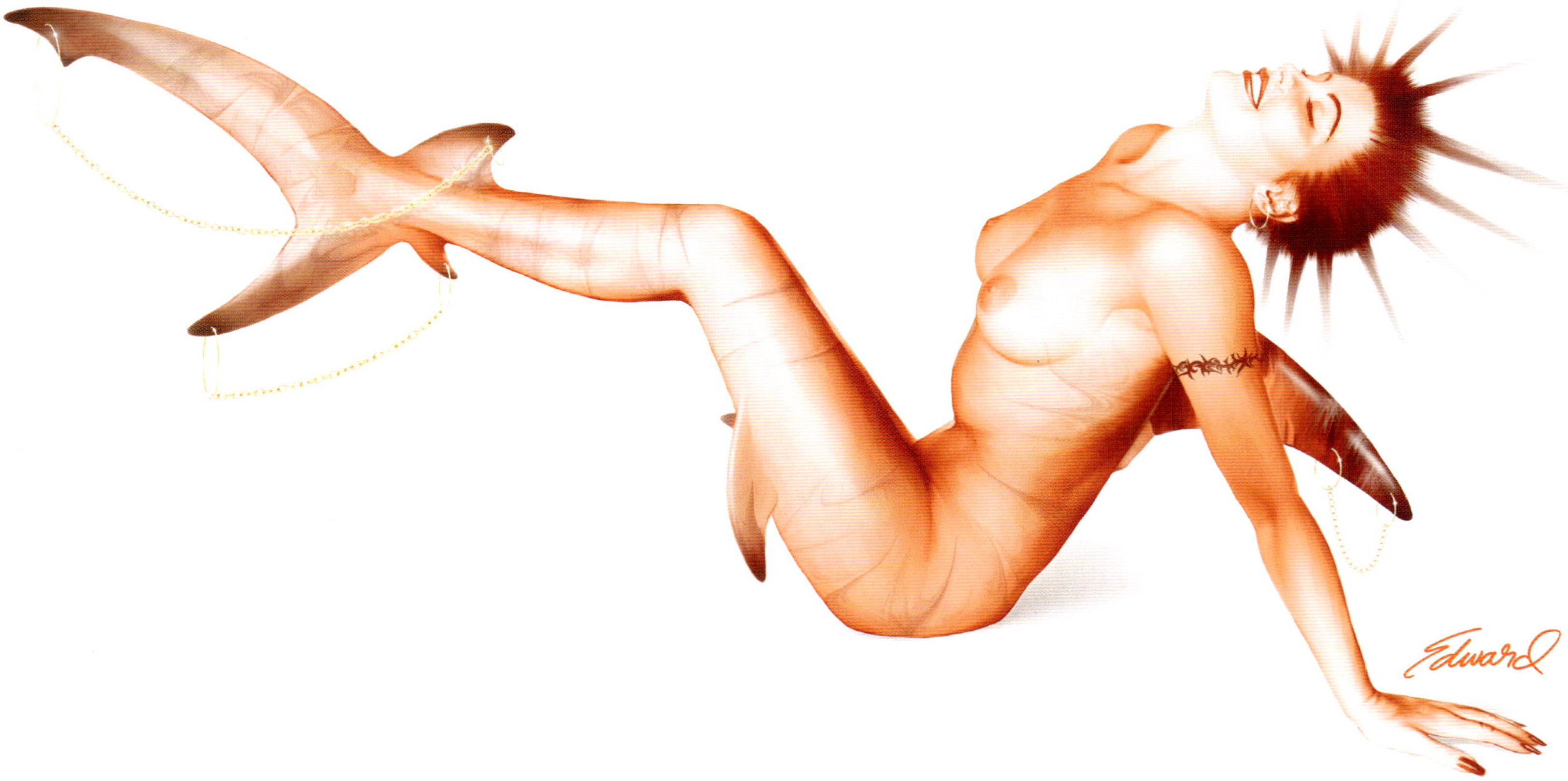

Sharkbait

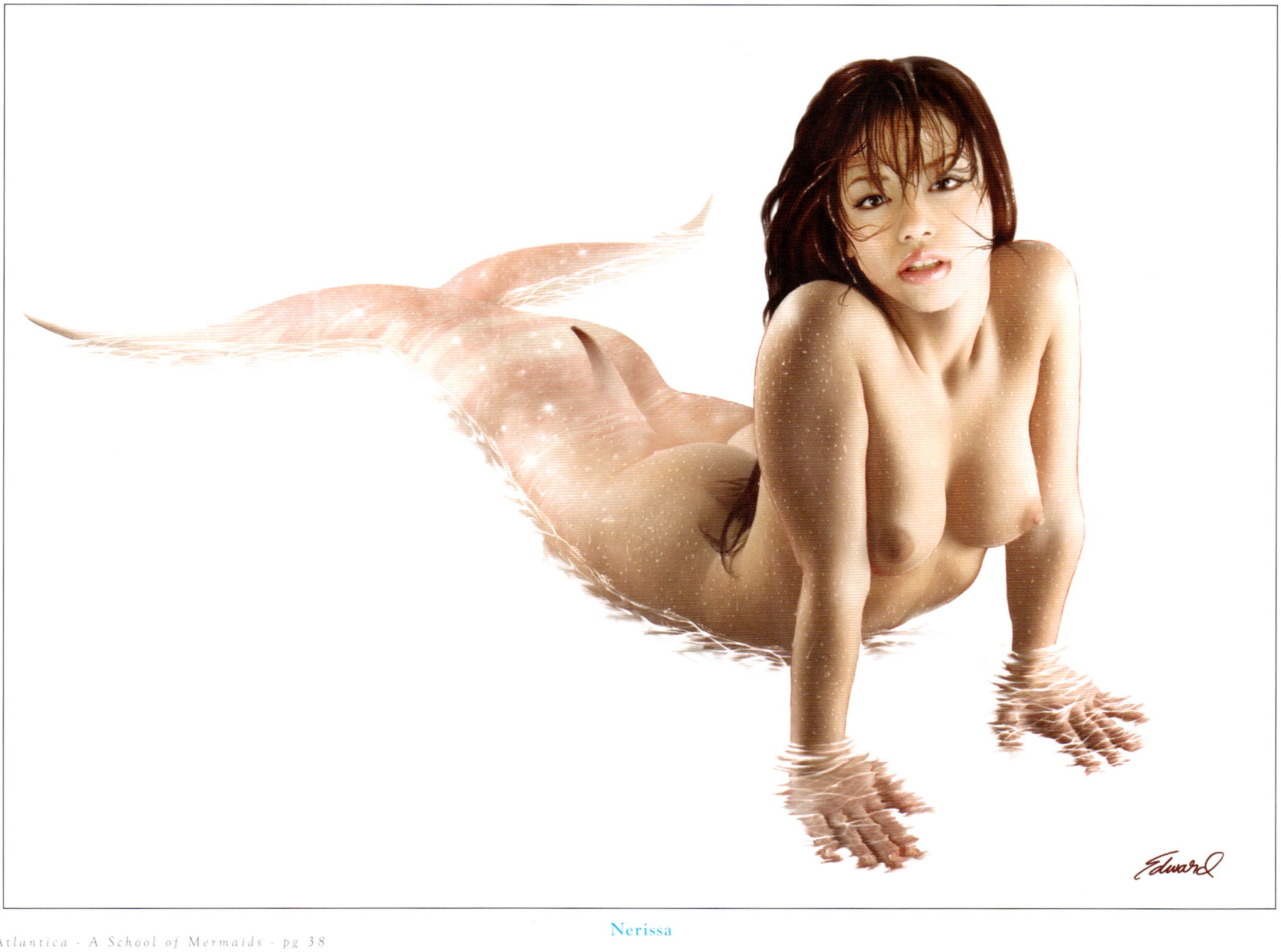

Nerissa

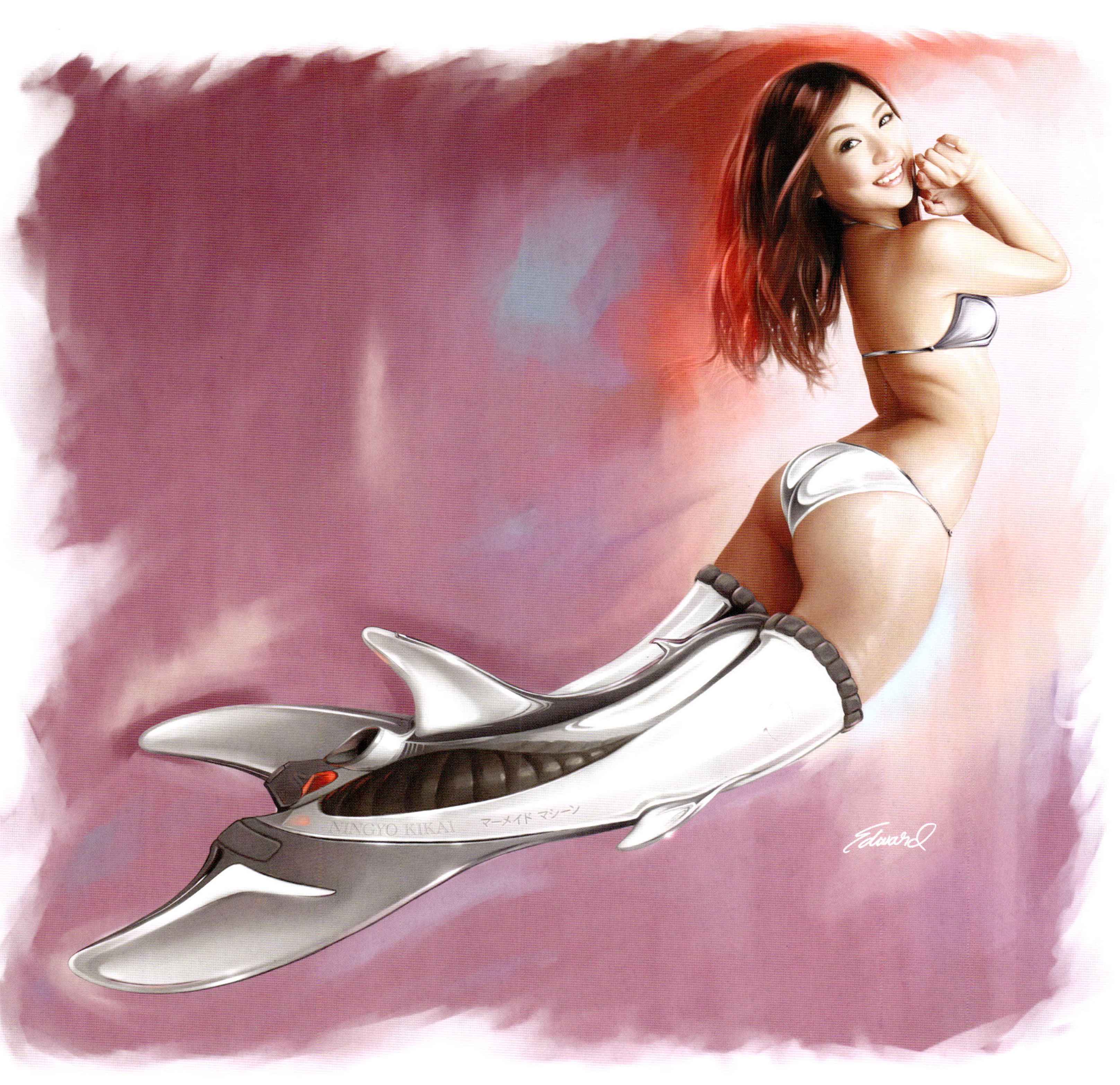

Mermaid Machine

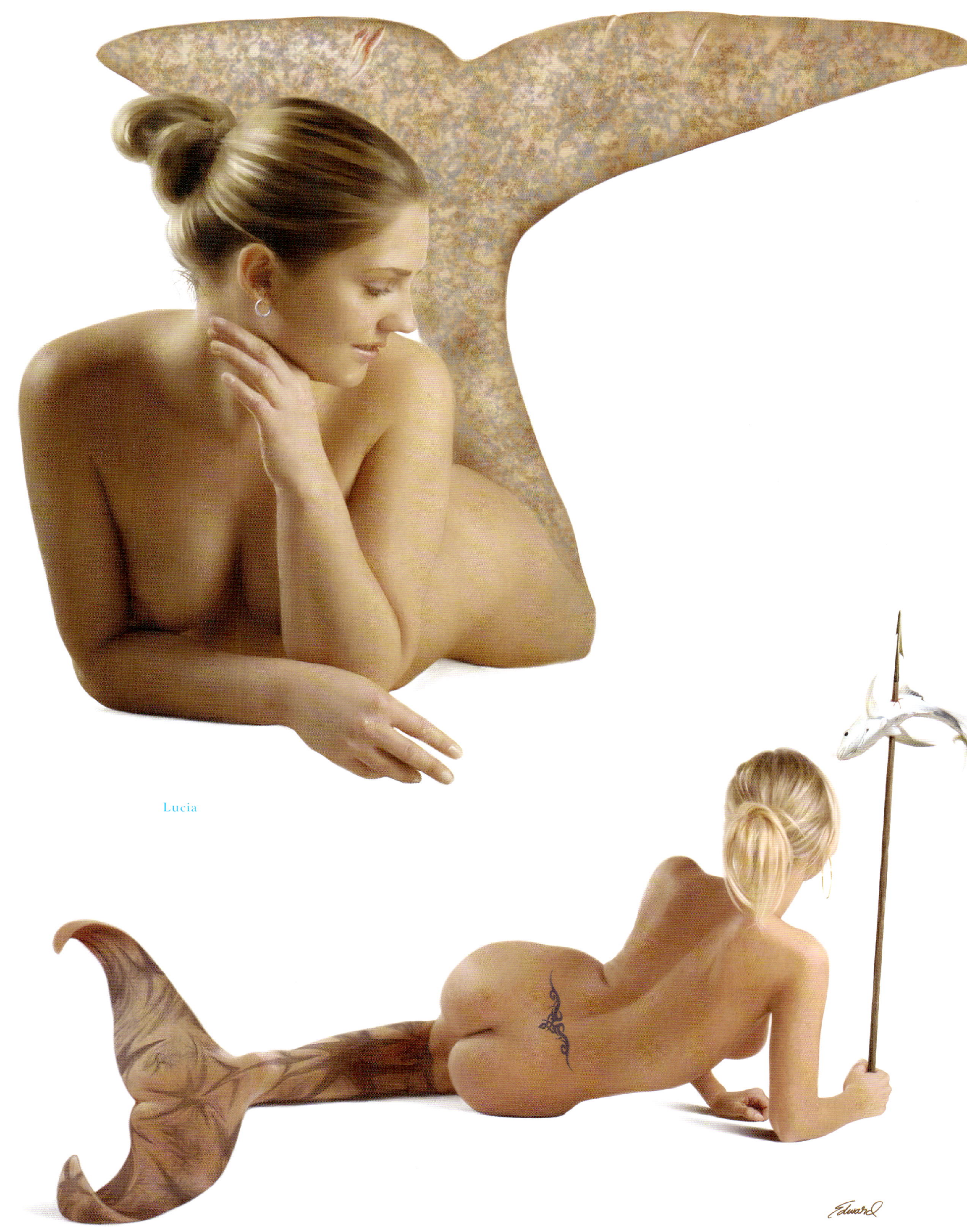

Lucia

Fish and Chips

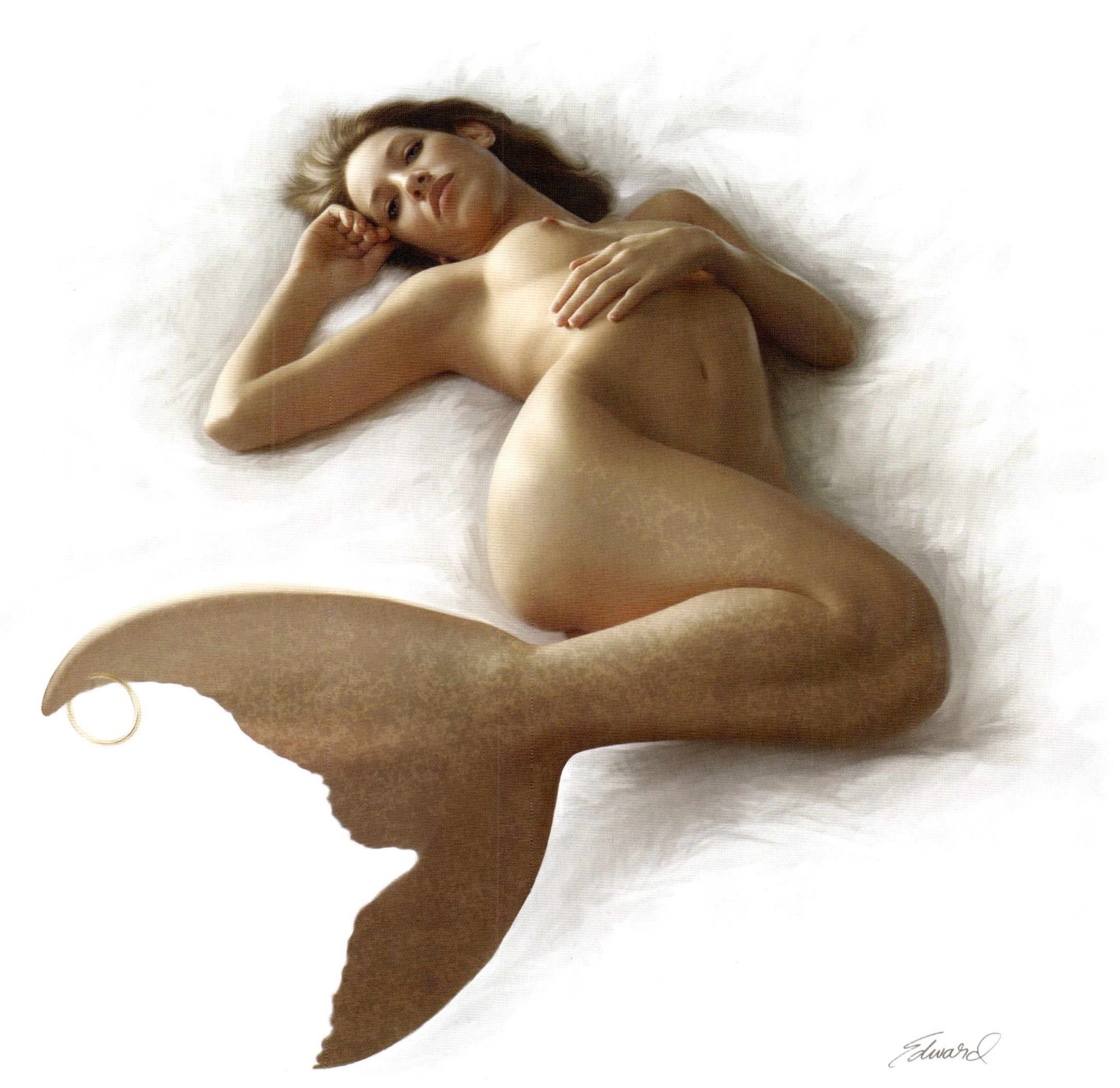

A Young Girl's Dreams

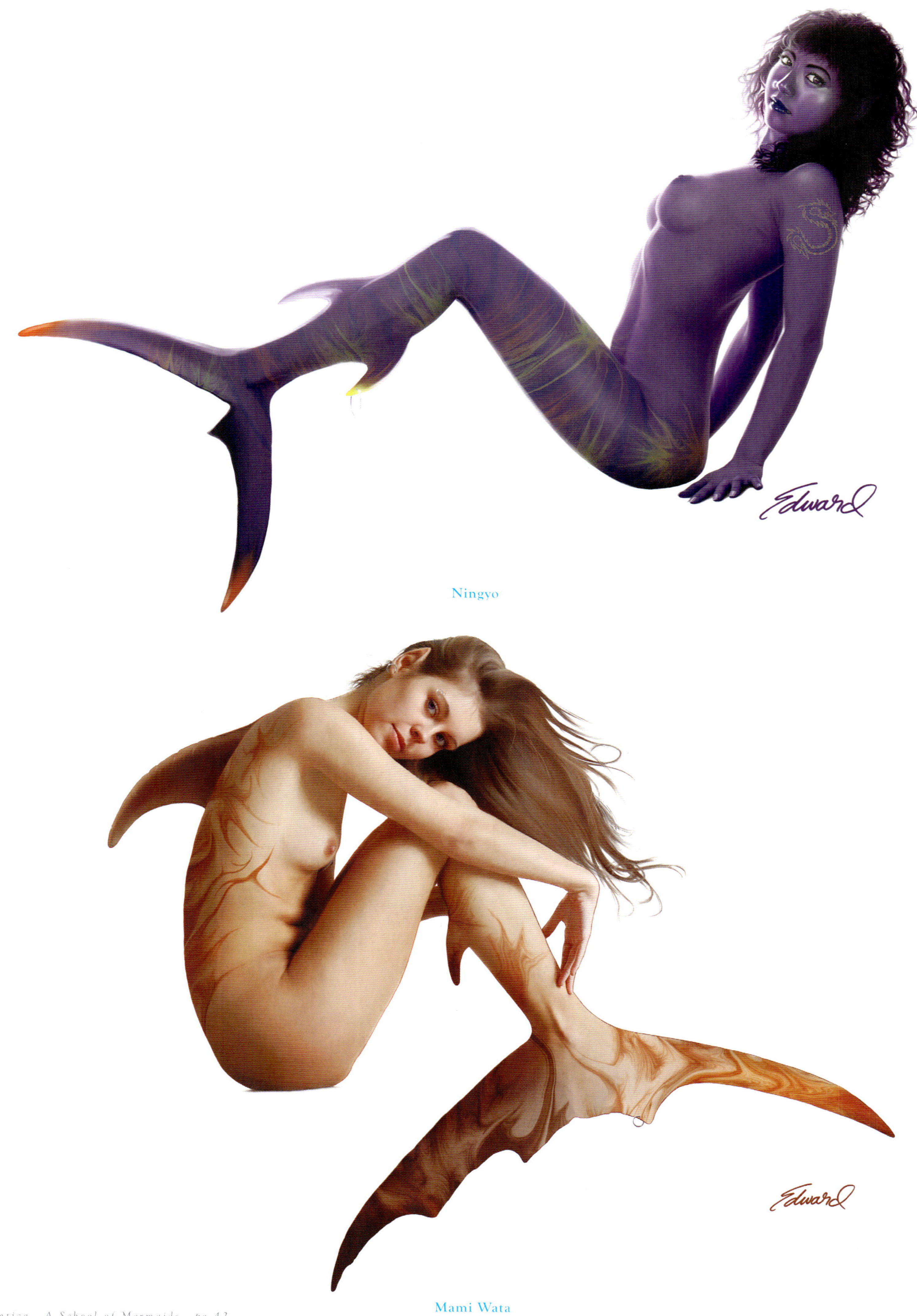

Ningyo

Mami Wata

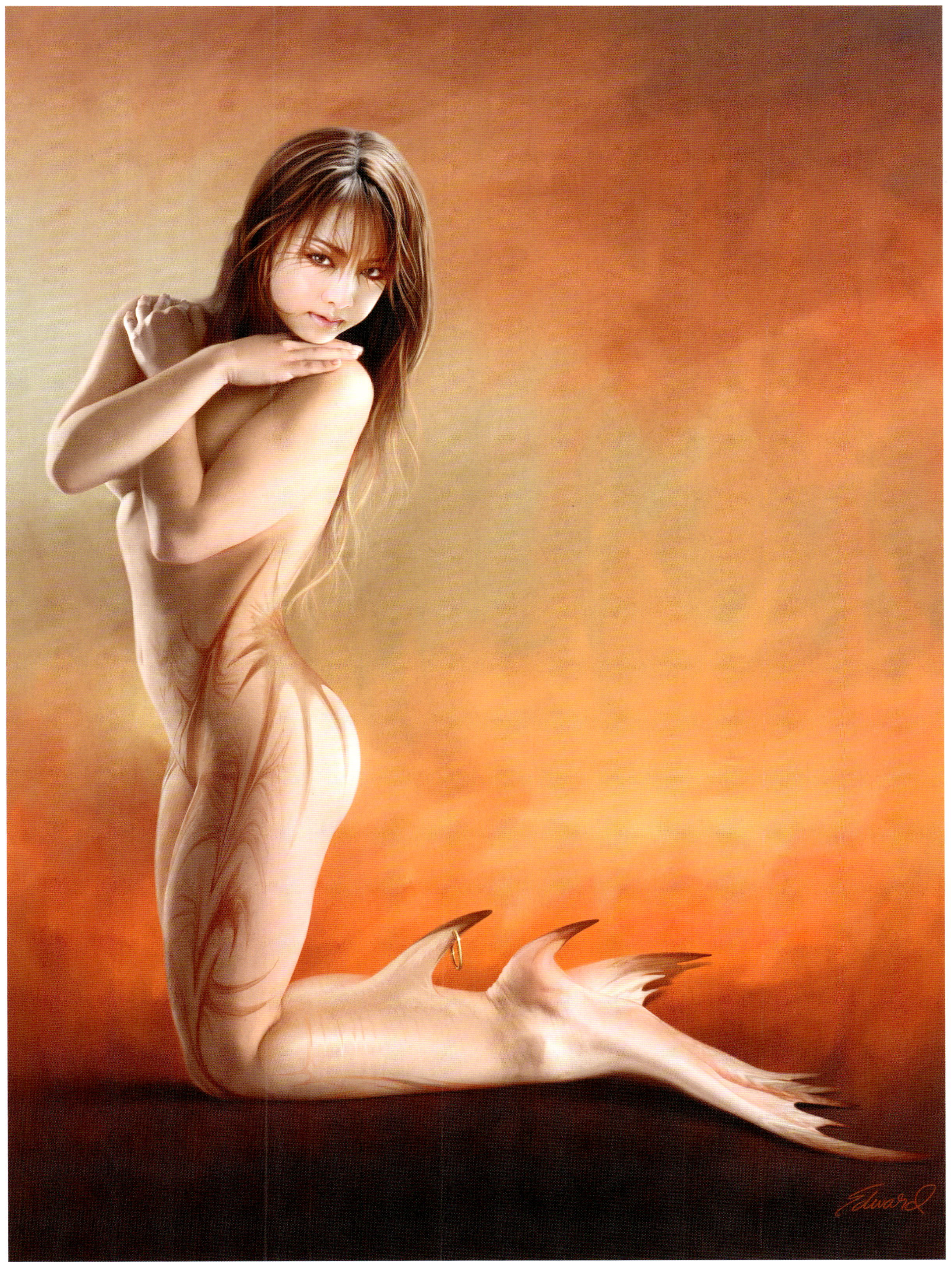

Atsui

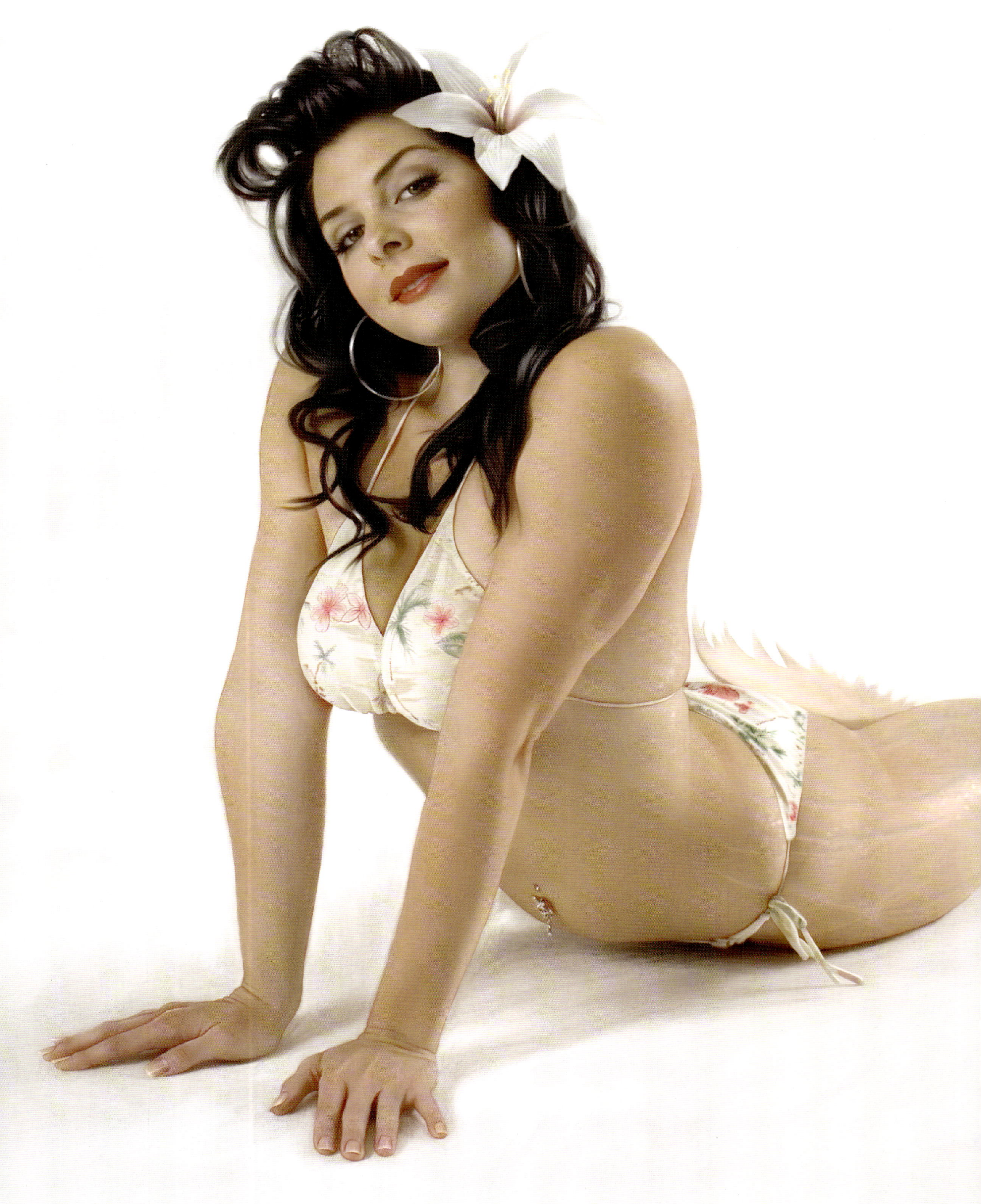

Ashley

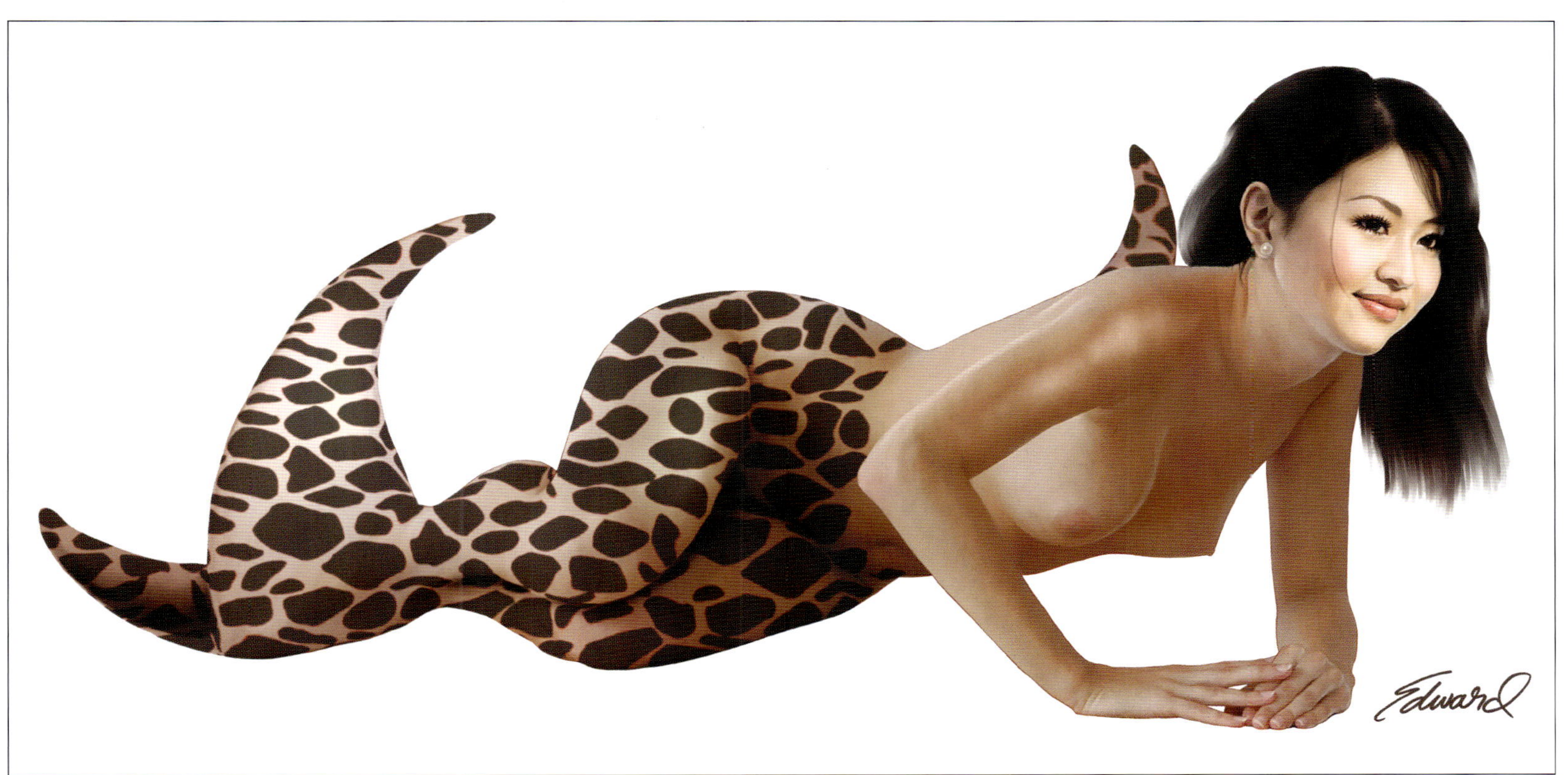

Oki

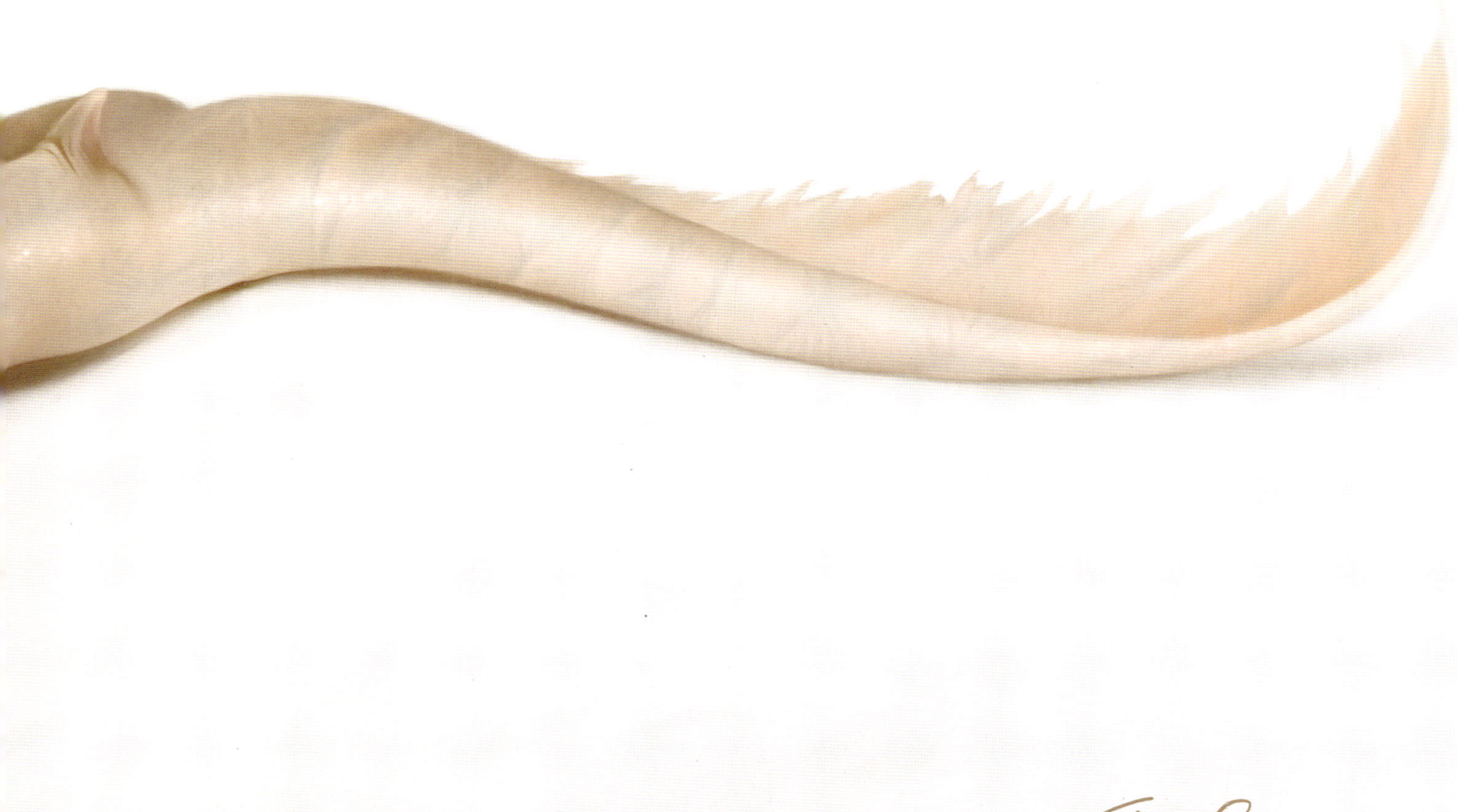

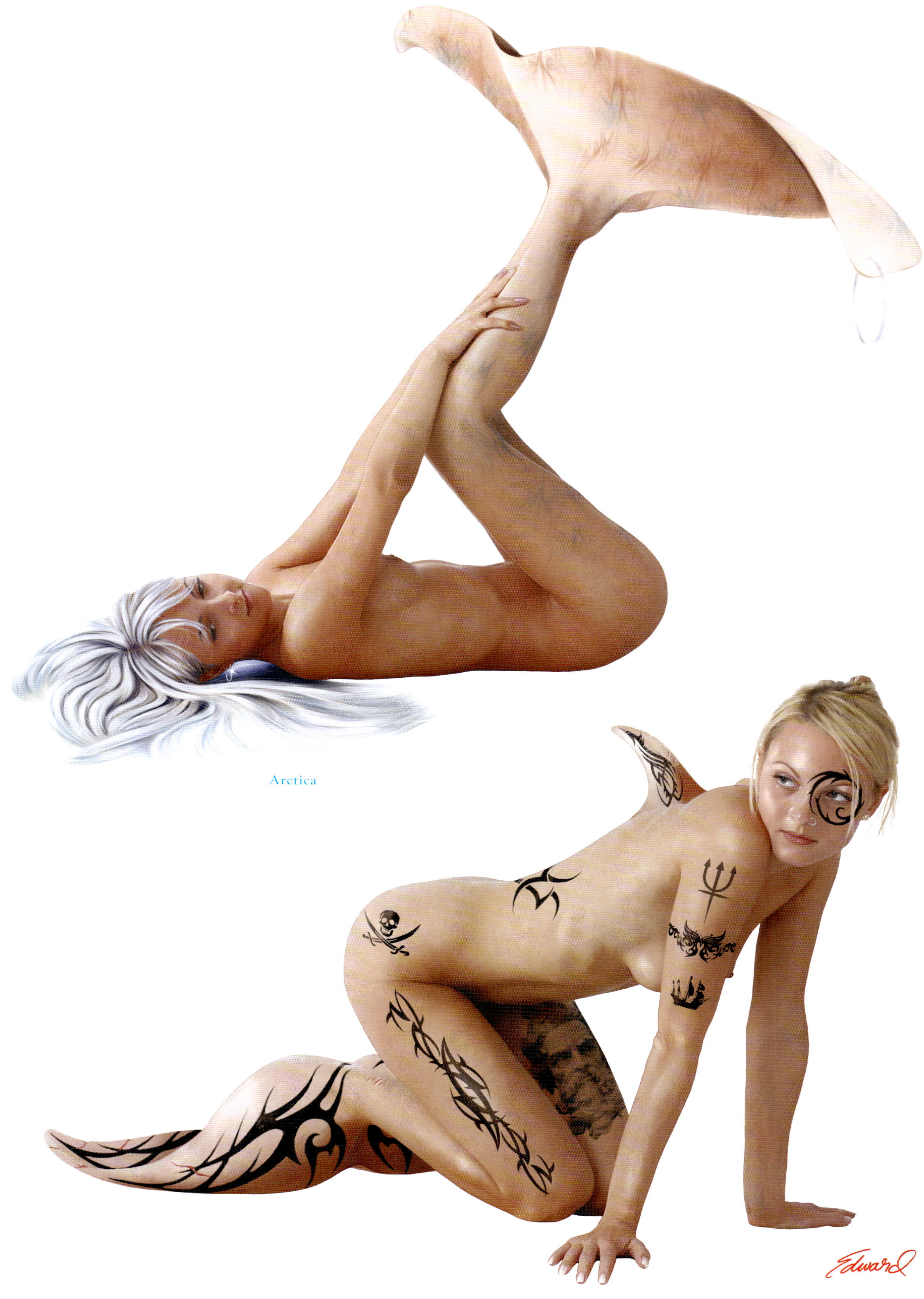

Arctica

Jolly Rhonda

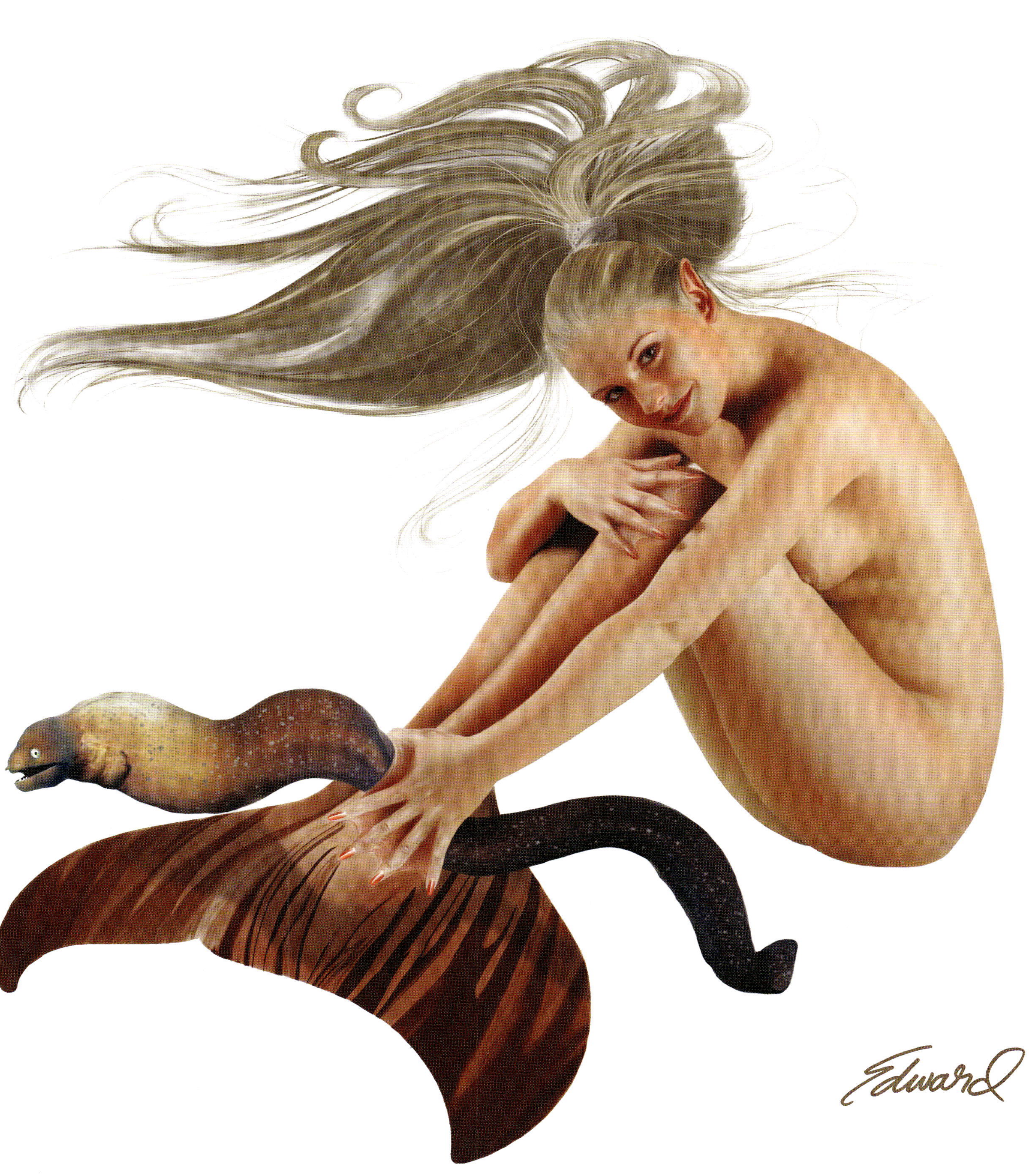

Lara

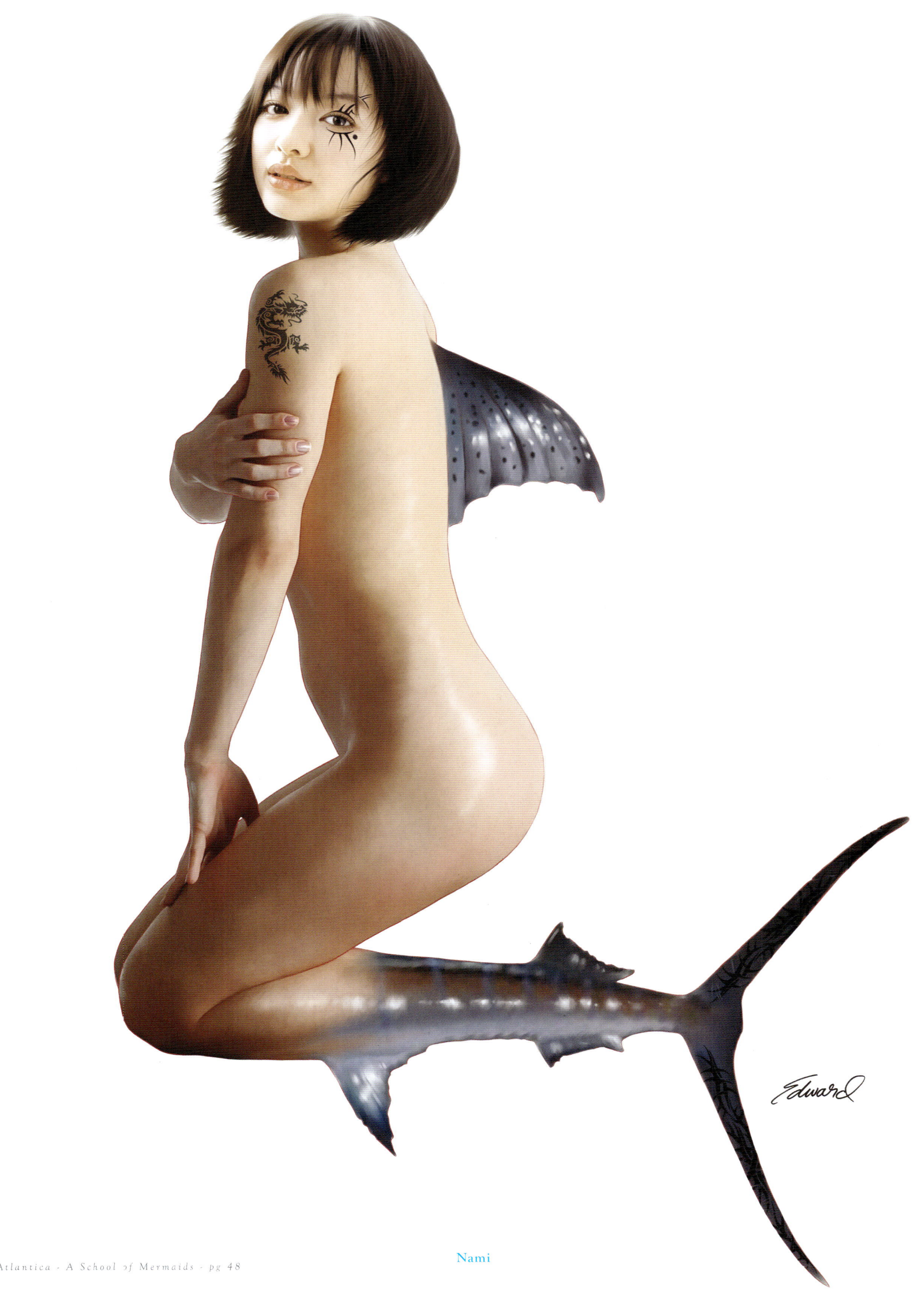

Nami